EDITED BY BARBARA IRELAND

The New York Times

HOURS
LOS ANGELES
& BEYOND

TASCHEN

Contents

Los Angeles

Angelenos like to tell visitors, "It's a great place to live but I wouldn't want to visit here." Granted, it's tough to decide what to see and do in a city that encompasses 470 square miles. Fortunately, there is always an under-the-radar restaurant, a funky theater, or a splashy store to discover. And you never have to leave the iconic landmarks behind. — BY LOUISE TUTELIAN

FRIDAY

1 *Stop and Shop* 4 p.m.

The hilly Los Feliz area, just northeast of Hollywood, is an old neighborhood with an impeccably hip pedigree. A walk along North Vermont Avenue turns up an intriguing trove of vintage clothes, handmade jewelry, antique textiles, books, and much more. **New High (M)Art** (1720 North Vermont Avenue; 323-638-0271; newhighmart.com), an industrial-style space filled with world music and the faint perfume of incense, stocks an eclectic mix. For sale one afternoon were a vintage French army camo jacket and a necklace made from hand-painted leather flags. **Skylight Books** (1818 North Vermont Avenue; 323-660-1175; skylightbooks.com) caters to the many artists, writers, musicians, and actors in the neighborhood — and anyone else who loves a carefully curated arts bookstore. Browse the stacks and you'll see a monograph on Richard Meier next to a tome on *Mad* magazine posters. And don't step on Franny, the resident cat.

2 *Friendly Fare* 6 p.m.

Little Dom's (2128 Hillhurst Avenue; 323-661-0055; littledoms.com; $$-$$$) is the best of homey and hip, a bar/bistro with an inventive menu. The fare is mostly Italian-American, but since the executive chef, Brandon Boudet, hails from New Orleans, there's a dash of the South as well. Pappardelle with house-made sausage? No problem. But Boudet also serves up a succulent fried oyster sandwich with hot sauce mayo, y'all.

3 *Bright Lights, Big City* 8 p.m.

Get the big picture at the **Griffith Park Observatory** (2800 East Observatory Avenue; 213-473-0800; griffithobservatory.org), with its view of the entire Los Angeles basin. Visitors line up for a peek into a massive Zeiss telescope with a 12-inch reflector that reveals celestial sights like the rings of Saturn. The Samuel Oschin Planetarium shows employ laser digital projection and state-of-the-art sound. A show about the brilliant aurora borealis — accompanied by Wagner's *Ride of the Valkyries* — is a cosmic experience.

4 *Alive and Swingin'* 10 p.m.

Made famous by the 1996 movie *Swingers*, the **Dresden** (1760 North Vermont Avenue; 323-665-4294; thedresden.com/lounge.html) is a welcome throwback to a still earlier era, with its upscale 1960s rec room décor and stellar bartenders. You're here to see Marty and Elayne, jazz musicians who have performed pop, standards, and the occasional show tune, with a changing array of guest artists, in the lounge since 1982. The crowd is a cocktail shaker of twenty-somethings on dates, middle-aged couples with friends, and college kids. Somehow, it all goes down very smoothly.

SATURDAY

5 *From Canyon to Canyon* 10 a.m.

Joni Mitchell doesn't live here anymore, but Laurel Canyon retains its '70s image as a

OPPOSITE The endless sprawl of Los Angeles. In a city of 470 square miles, there's always something to do.

BELOW At the Griffith Park Observatory, stargazers line up for a peek at celestial sights like the rings of Saturn.

self-contained artistic enclave (albeit a more expensive one now). Its social hub is the **Canyon Country Store** (2108 Laurel Canyon Boulevard; 323-654-8091), a grocery/deli/liquor store marked by a flower power-style sign that pays homage to its hippie roots. Sip organic oak-roasted espresso at the Canyon Coffee Cart, buy a picnic lunch, and head for the high road — Mulholland Drive.

ABOVE Skylight Books in Los Feliz, just northeast of Hollywood, caters to writers, artists, musicians, and actors.

BELOW The crowd at the Dresden, where Marty and Elayne perform on weekends, is a cocktail shaker of 20-somethings on dates, clumps of middle-aged friends, and college kids.

The serpentine road follows the ridgeline of the Santa Monica Mountains, and every curve delivers a spectacular vista of the San Fernando Valley and beyond. Drop down into **Franklin Canyon Park** (2600 Franklin Canyon Drive; 310-858-7272; lamountains.com), 605 acres of chaparral, grass-lands, and oak woodlands with miles of hiking grounds. Heavenly Pond is a particularly appealing picnic spot.

6 *The Hills of Beverly* 1 p.m.

The stores range from Gap to Gucci, but you don't need deep pockets to enjoy Beverly Hills. **Prada** (343 North Rodeo Drive; 310-278-8661; prada.com), designed by Rem Koolhaas, delivers a jolt of architectural electricity. The 50-foot entrance is wide open to the street, with no door (and no name, either). A staircase peopled with mannequins ascends mysteriously. On the top level, faux security scanners double as video monitors and luggage-carousel-style shelves hold merchandise. At the **Paley Center for Media** (465 North Beverly Drive; 310-786-1091; paleycenter.org/visit-visitla), enter your own private TVland. At the center's library, anyone can screen segments of classic TV and radio shows, from *The Three Stooges* to *Seinfeld* as well as documentaries and specials. When it's time to cool your heels, head for the **Beverly Canon Gardens** (241 North Canon Drive), a public park masquerading

as a private Italian-style garden. Adjacent to the Montage Hotel, the Gardens have plenty of benches, tables, and chairs, and a large Baroque fountain adding a splashing soundtrack.

7 *Full Exposure* 4 p.m.

The incongruous setting of corporate high-rises is home to the under-appreciated **Annenberg Space for Photography** (2000 Avenue of the Stars; 213-403-3000; annenbergspaceforphotography.org), an oasis of images. One enthralling group show was by nature photographers shooting under Arctic oceans, on a volcano, and deep within Florida swamps. Another featured photographs by Herb Ritts, Mary Ellen Mark, Chuck Close, and other documentarians of beauty and style. The space itself is open and airy, with an iris-like design on the ceiling to represent the aperture of a lens.

8 *Unleashed* 6 p.m.

Don't knock it till you've tried it. Only a restaurant unequivocally named **Animal** (435 North Fairfax Avenue; 323-782-9225; animalrestaurant.com; $$-$$$) can sell diners on dishes like pig ear with chili, lime, and a fried egg, or rabbit legs with mustard and bacon. A longstanding landmark of the snout-to-tail culinary revival, the place is nondescript with no name on the storefront (it's four doors up from Canter's Deli), but once you've tried the fat

pork-belly sliders with crunchy slaw on a buttery brioche bun, you'll beat a path there again.

9 *The Silent Treatment* 8 p.m.

Dedicated to finding, screening, and conserving unusual films (can you say, *"Killer Klowns From Outer Space"*?), the 120-seat **Silent Movie Theater** (611 North Fairfax Avenue; 323-655-2510; cinefamily.org) is like a quirky film class held in a club. Where else can you claim a well-worn couch and pour a cocktail from a punch bowl while waiting for show time? Insider tip: Regulars bring their own bottles of wine.

SUNDAY

10 *Breakfast by the Beach* 10 a.m.

Berries and Brussels sprouts abound at the **Santa Monica Farmers' Market** (2640 Main Street; Santa Monica; 310-458-8712; smgov.net/portals/farmersmarket), but there are also 10 stands where local restaurateurs sell dishes prepared on the spot. Among the best are Arcadie's sweet or savory crepes, Carbon Grill's hefty burritos, and

ABOVE Basking poolside at the eco-chic Palomar boutique hotel on Wilshire Boulevard, near the University of California at Los Angeles.

the Victorian's custom omelets. A live band might be playing any genre from jazz to zydeco. Finish with a scone from the Rockenwagner bakery stand and munch it on the beach, only a block away.

11 *Secret Waterways* 1 p.m.
One of the loveliest walks in west Los Angeles is one visitors hardly ever take: a stroll among the **Venice canals**. The developer Abbot Kinney dug miles of canals in 1905 to create his vision of a

Venice in America. The decades took their toll, but the remaining canals were drained and refurbished in 1993. The surrounding neighborhood is now on the National Register of Historic Places. Charming footpaths crisscross the canals as ducks splash underneath. On the banks, mansions stand next to small bungalows. Residents pull kayaks and canoes up to their homes. It's quiet, serene, and hidden. Hollywood? Where's that?

ABOVE Spindly palms and an evening sky in Los Feliz.

OPPOSITE Despite its high rises and packed freeways, Los Angeles has room for places that can feel remote, like this trail in the Santa Monica Mountains.

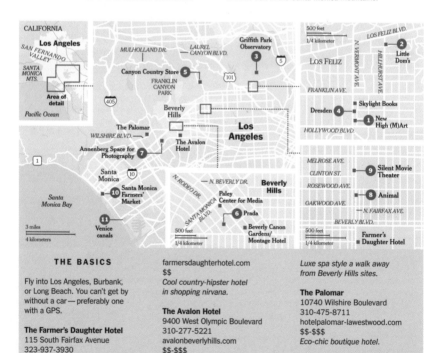

THE BASICS

Fly into Los Angeles, Burbank, or Long Beach. You can't get by without a car—preferably one with a GPS.

The Farmer's Daughter Hotel
115 South Fairfax Avenue
323-937-3930

farmersdaughterhotel.com
$$
Cool country-hipster hotel in shopping nirvana.

The Avalon Hotel
9400 West Olympic Boulevard
310-277-5221
avalonbeverlyhills.com
$$-$$$

Luxe spa style a walk away from Beverly Hills sites.

The Palomar
10740 Wilshire Boulevard
310-475-8711
hotelpalomar-lawestwood.com
$$-$$$
Eco-chic boutique hotel.

Downtown Los Angeles

The sprawl, the scale, all that freeway time—for many, Los Angeles is an acquired taste. But not downtown. New York-like in its density and mishmash, the long-blighted center has become an accessible, pedestrian-friendly destination in recent years; Angelenos walk around en masse, using their actual legs. The immense L.A. Live entertainment complex is largely responsible for this comeback, but the studiously vintage bars and imaginative restaurants that seem to open every other day are also part of the revival. Skid Row and the drifts of homeless camps haven't vanished altogether, and the grittiness still varies by block. But this part of town is alive again, in ways that make sense even to an outsider.
— BY CHRIS COLIN

FRIDAY

1 *Do the Crawl* 4 p.m.

The Downtown Art Walk — a party-in-the-streets bonanza that draws thousands of revelers the second Thursday of every month — is one way to experience the area's robust art scene. But you can do your own art walk anytime, and you should. Lured by low rents, a number of impressive galleries have found a home here, many of them on Chung King Road, a pedestrian alley strung with lanterns in Chinatown. For starters, look in at **Charlie James Gallery** (No. 969; 213-687-0844; cjamesgallery.com), **Coagula Curatorial** (No. 974; 424-226-2485; coagulacuratorial.com), and **Gregorio Escalante Gallery** (No. 978; 323-697-8728; gregorioescalante.com). The shows are intimate and occasionally provocative, featuring a broad array of contemporary artists: William Powhida, Orly Cogan, and others.

2 *The City at Its Brightest* 7:30 p.m.

Whether you're catching a Lakers game, touring the Grammy Museum, or attending a concert at the Nokia Theater, there is always something

splashy to do at the 27-acre, $2.5 billion sports and entertainment behemoth that is **L.A. Live** (800 West Olympic Boulevard; 213-763-5483; lalive.com). Just strolling the Tokyo-ish Nokia Plaza — 20,000 square feet of LED signage — is diverting. An array of restaurants and bars is clustered at the periphery, but many visitors prefer just to stroll around this giant pedestrian zone, trying to take it all in.

3 *A Late, Great Bite* 10 p.m.

The Gorbals (216 Fifth Street; 213-488-3408; $$) is one of the more fantastic — and odd — downtown dining options. The chef and owner, a previous Top Chef winner, is part Scottish and part Israeli, and his hybrid concoctions are terrific. On one visit, banh mi poutine merged Quebec and Vietnam in ways criminally neglected until now. Bacon-wrapped matzo balls, anyone? The restaurant moved from its original quarters in an old downtown hotel, but it retained perhaps its best menu item: for $10, you can buy the kitchen staff a round of beers.

SATURDAY

4 *On the Nickel* 9 a.m.

The maple bacon doughnut is a stand-out on the breakfast menu at the new but ageless **Nickel Diner** (524 South Main Street; 213-623-8301; nickeldiner.com; $). The rest is mostly well-executed diner food. What's remarkable is the location — until recently, this block was one of Skid Row's most notorious. It's a testament to downtown's revival that the intersection of Main

OPPOSITE Broadway in downtown Los Angeles, a pedestrian-friendly destination rebounding from 20th-century decline.

RIGHT Fabric in the Fashion District, a 100-block mix of wholesale-only shops and designer retail discounts.

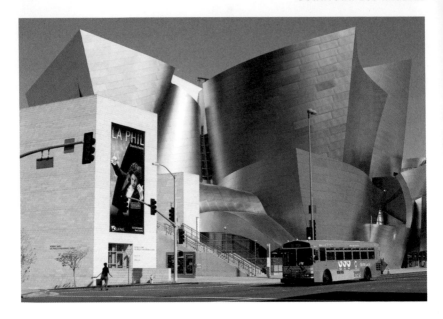

and Fifth (hence "Nickel") is now home to a place where people line up for tables.

5 *Nice Threads* 10:30 a.m.

The 100-block **Fashion District** mixes high and low seamlessly. Though many shops sell wholesale only, you can still find a wide selection of deeply discounted designer clothes, fabric, and accessories. The jumbled shops and warehouses at Ninth and Los Angeles Streets are a start (feel free to bargain). Don't miss the rowdier **Santee Alley** (thesanteealley.com), a chaotic open-air bazaar where cheap meets weird in a thoroughly Los Angeles way. Energetic vendors hawk the impressive (perfect knock-off handbags) and the odd (toy frogs emblazoned with gang insignias). Find a higher-end experience around the corner at **Acne Studios** (855 South Broadway; 213-243-0960; acnestudios.com/stores/s-broadway), a branch of a Swedish fashion brand. Dripping with 21st-century cool, it draws shoppers to the Art Deco spaces of the

ABOVE Find the outdoor stairway on Frank Gehry's Walt Disney Concert Hall and climb its curves to a rooftop garden.

OPPOSITE ABOVE Drinks at Seven Grand, one of the retro bars inspired by downtown's colorful history.

OPPOSITE BELOW The Nickel Diner, a busy spot in a revived area that not so long ago was part of Skid Row.

Eastern Columbia Building. For an expedition tailored to your particular agenda, contact **Urban Shopping Adventures** (213-683-9715) for a guided shopping trip.

6 *Accessible Architecture* 1 p.m.

The arrival of the conductor Gustavo Dudamel at the Los Angeles Philharmonic has brought new crowds to the symphony, but the **Walt Disney Concert Hall** (111 South Grand Avenue; 323-850-2000; laphil.com) — Frank Gehry's deconstructivist celebration of all that is big, curvy, and shiny — deserves a visit even without a ticket. Bring a picnic and wind your way along the semi-hidden outer staircase up to an excellent city vista and rooftop garden oasis. Free guided tours and self-guided audio tours are available most days. Check first (musiccenter.org) for schedules.

7 *Lazy Bones* 7 p.m.

Since 2010, **Lazy Ox Canteen** (241 South San Pedro Street; 213-626-5299; lazyoxcanteen.com; $$-$$$) in Little Tokyo has been the kind of tucked-away gastropub people love to insist is the city's best. Casual and buzzing, the bistro has a long menu featuring adventurous delicacies, from trotters to crispy pigs' ears to lamb neck hash. It's hard to pin the cuisine to a specific origin, but a penchant for bold, meat-centric comfort food is evident. Get several small plates.

8 *Pick a Show, Any Show* 8:30 p.m.

If you're downtown for a performance, chances are it's a sprawling affair at L.A. Live. But a handful of smaller settings offer funkier alternatives. The **Redcat Theater** (631 West Second Street; 213-237-2800; redcat.org) plays host to all manner of experimental performances — one Saturday in winter featured theater, dance, puppetry, and live music from a Slovene-Latvian art collaboration. **Club Mayan** (1038 South Hill Street; 213-746-4287; clubmayan.com), an ornate old dance club most nights, occasionally hosts mad events like Lucha VaVoom, which combines burlesque and Mexican wrestling. And the **Smell** (247 South Main Street; thesmell.org), a likably grimy, volunteer-run space, hosts very small bands circled by swaying teenagers.

9 *Drink as if It's Illegal* 10:30 p.m.

Was Los Angeles a hoot during Prohibition? No need to guess, thanks to a slew of meticulously old-timey new bars that exploit the wonderful history of old Los Angeles. From upscale speakeasy (the **Varnish**; 118 East Sixth Street; 213-622-9999; thevarnishbar.com) to converted-power-plant chic (the **Edison**; 108 West Second Street; 213-613-0000; edisondowntown.com) to an old bank vault (the **Crocker Club**; 453 South Spring Street; 213-239-9099; crockerclub.com), these spiffy places do set decoration as only Los Angeles can. And fussily delicious artisanal cocktails are as plentiful as you'd imagine. The well-scrubbed will also enjoy the swanky **Seven Grand** (515 West Seventh Street, second floor; 213-614-0737; sevengrandbars.com), while the well-scuffed may feel more at home at **La Cita Bar** (336 South Hill Street; 213-687-7111; lacitabar.com).

SUNDAY

10 *Big Art* 11 a.m.

Contemporary art galleries are de rigueur, but Los Angeles was in the vanguard. Its **Museum of Contemporary Art** (main location, 250 South Grand Avenue; 213-626-6222; moca.org), opened in 1979. Stop in to see what's behind its reputation for a fine collection and exciting special exhibitions.

11 *Broad Art* 1 p.m.

Cross the street for a cool take on Sunday brunch (Otium restaurant, otiumla.com; $$) and an even more contemporary view of contemporary art, both at **The Broad** (221 South Grand Avenue; 213-232-6200; thebroad.org). The Los Angeles philanthropists Eli and Edythe Broad (pronounced brode), who have long supported the arts and the development of the Grand Avenue Arts District, opened this museum in 2015 to display their own extensive art collection. The honeycombed facade is striking, and works inside range from Andy Warhol to Jeff Koons and up-to-the-minute multimedia pieces.

ABOVE If an art piece is much older than the first baby boomer, you're not likely to find it in the Museum of Contemporary Art, which is rich in works by Rothko, Oldenburg, Lichtenstein, and Rauschenberg.

OPPOSITE Downtown skyscrapers aglow in the Los Angeles night. About half a million people go to work every day in downtown's clusters of office towers and civic buildings. In the off hours, it's now also a place to play.

THE BASICS

Walking works better than it used to, but you may still want a car.

Ritz-Carlton
900 West Olympic Boulevard
213-743-8800
lalive.com/stay/ritzcarlton
$$$$
Half of a gleaming new two-hotel complex rising above L.A. Live.

JW Marriott
900 West Olympic Boulevard
213-765-8600
lalive.com/stay/jwmarriott
$$-$$$
The other half of the same hotel complex.

Ace Hotel Downtown Los Angeles
929 South Broadway
213-623-3233
acehotel.com/losangeles
$$$
Hipster update of 1920s building with movie palace still inside.

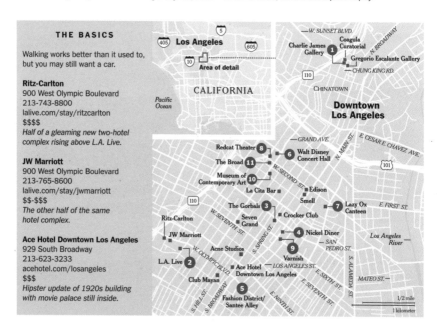

Hollywood

Hollywood is one of those rare places that live up to their stereotypes, right down to the sign. But with minimal effort, it can offer a whole lot more. This pedestrian-friendly district represents both Los Angeles's past, with icons like the Capitol Records building, and the city's future—multi-ethnic, vertical, dense. A recent renaissance means there are now million-dollar condos, trendy restaurants, celebrity watering holes, and a world-class movie theater. But there are still tattoo parlors, sex shops, and homelessness. Tying it all together is the Hollywood Walk of Fame, where it is hard not to be at least momentarily tickled (Hello, Mister Rogers) or merely confused (Who the heck was that?). It remains a place that only Los Angeles could produce.
— BY JENNIFER STEINHAUER

FRIDAY

1 *Costume Change* 4 p.m.

Before you unpack your bags, prepare to fill them up. Hollywood is awash in vintage clothing stores, many of them filled with remnants from television and movie sets past. **Golyester** (450 South La Brea Avenue; 323-931-1339; golyester.com) has amazingly preserved purses, negligees ($278 was the price for one two-piece Christian Dior number), gowns (on one visit, a white leather dress with fur trim) and more. Of special interest are the shoes—finds like gold sling-backs, emerald stilettos, or elegant Herbert Levine pumps. Down the street is **The Way We Wore** (334 South La Brea Avenue; 323-937-0878; thewaywewore.com) with more vintage treasures. Keep going to **Cafe Midi** (148 South La Brea Avenue; 323-939-9860; cafemidi. com), where you can have a cappuccino and take in the Moroccan ceramic bowls and candles in the adjacent store.

2 *Planet Thai* 7:30 p.m.

There are upscale bistros and giant tuna rolls aplenty in the neighborhood, but Angelenos love Hollywood for Thai food. Reasonable minds can quibble over the best, which tends to be high on authentic flair, low on atmosphere, and budget-priced. Good examples are the **Sapp Coffee Shop** (5183 Hollywood Boulevard; 323-665-1035) and

Ruen Pair (5257 Hollywood Boulevard; 323-466-0153). For a slightly more upscale ambience, check out **Bulan Thai Vegetarian Kitchen** (7168 Melrose Avenue; 323-857-1882; bulanthai.com), a chic spot that's hot with the yoga crowd. Look for menu items like busaba pumpkin, mock duck curry, and mushroom tom kah.

3 *Hockney Night* 10 p.m.

Nothing is more echt Hollywood than the **Tropicana Pool** (7000 Hollywood Boulevard; 323-466-7000; hollywoodroosevelt.com), nestled beneath tall palms at the Hollywood Roosevelt Hotel. The pool and its louche cocktail bar have played host to Clark Gable and Marilyn Monroe, and celebrity sightings are still common. But the real treat is the pool itself. At night it's covered with translucent flooring, enabling you to sip cocktails while admiring the abstract underwater mural painted by David Hockney.

SATURDAY

4 *Is That Tom Cruise?* 8:30 a.m.

Los Angeles is a morning town, so get going at **Square One Dining** (4854 Fountain Avenue; 323-661-1109; squareonedining.com; $$), a cheerful local spot that focuses on farmers' market produce.

OPPOSITE The evening lights near Sunset Boulevard.

BELOW From behind the famous Hollywood sign, the glittering lights below promise a world of celebrities, mansions, palm tree-lined boulevards, and movie studios.

Order some French toast with banana citrus caramel or the transporting pressed egg sandwich with tomato and arugula. Stare at the Scientology headquarters across the street, among the more relevant fixtures in Hollywood, and try to see who is going in and coming out of its parking structure.

5 *Open House* 11 a.m.

Many a native Angeleno knows not of **Barnsdall Art Park** (4800 Hollywood Boulevard; 323-660-4254; barnsdallartpark.com), a public space donated to the city by the eccentric Aline Barnsdall in 1927. Beyond having one of the best views of the Hollywood sign and grass upon which to sit (a rare thing in Los Angeles), the site is home to the **Los Angeles Municipal Art Gallery**, a theater, and Frank Lloyd Wright's first Los Angeles project, the **Hollyhock House** (323-913-4030; barnsdall.org/hollyhock-house). Tours of the house begin at 12:30 p.m.

6 *Food (and Music) for the Soul* 2 p.m.

You thought you went to Hollywood to eat raw food? That's West Hollywood. Before your afternoon walking tour, load up on carbs at **Roscoe's House of Chicken and Waffles** (1514 North Gower Street; 323-466-7453; roscoeschickenandwaffles.com; $-$$). The beloved soul food chain is known for its half chicken smothered with gravy and served with two waffles. From Roscoe's, it's a fast walk to **Amoeba Records** (6400 Sunset Boulevard; 323-245-6400; amoeba.com), one of the last great independent record stores in the country, where new and used CDs and DVDs are found by the mile. There are also live in-store performances (with a special emphasis on up-and-coming Los Angeles bands).

7 *High-Tech Movie* 5 p.m.

Keep walking. Now you are headed to the **ArcLight Cinema** (6360 West Sunset Boulevard; 323-464-1478; arclightcinemas.com), which has one of the best projection and sound systems in the country, plus comfy chairs. Catch the latest popcorn

flick, obscure retrospective, or independent picture with every serious cinema buff in town.

8 *Peru in Hollywood* 8 p.m.

Turn the corner on North Vine, and end up in a tiny spot where the spare décor is made up of small replicas of Lima's famous balcones, or balconies. Known for its ceviches, **Los Balcones del Peru** (1360 North Vine Street; 323-871-9600; $) is a charming restaurant, down the block from a pawn shop, where families, couples, and guys who prefer a place on one of the tiger-patterned bar stools all feed. Start with chicha morada (a fruit drink made with corn water), then hit the lomo saltado (beef sautéed with onions) or tacu tacu con mariscos (refried Peruvian beans with shrimp).

9 *Dark Nights* 11 p.m.

End the evening at the **Woods** (1533 North La Brea Avenue; 323-876-6612; vintagebargroup.com/the-woods.php), which, as the name implies, has an outdoorsy theme. The sleek bar has lots of cedar and elk antler chandeliers hanging from the star-encrusted ceiling. As you scope out the young crowd and peruse the juke box, have one of the signature mint juleps or a seasonal drink like the pumpkin pie shot.

SUNDAY

10 *Celebrity Dog Walkers* 9:30 a.m.

Two blocks north of Hollywood Boulevard is one of the most scenic, unusual urban parks in the country, **Runyon Canyon**. The 130-acre park offers steep, invigorating hikes with views of the San

Fernando Valley, the Pacific, Catalina Island (on clear days), and the Griffith Observatory. The area is popular with dog owners (including celebrities), who take advantage of the leash-free policy. Mixed in among the wild chaparral are the crumbling estates of Carman Runyon, a coal magnate who used the property for hunting, and George Huntington Hartford II, heir to the A&P fortune. Parking can be tricky, so enter from the north, off Mulholland. You'll find a parking lot and start the hike going downhill.

11 *Walk This Way* Noon

You can't leave Hollywood without strolling down Hollywood Boulevard on the **Hollywood Walk of Fame** (hollywoodchamber.net). Take in the hundreds of stars embedded in the sidewalks, just

to see how many you recognize. While so doing, stop at **Lucky Devils** (6613 Hollywood Boulevard; 323-465-8259) for a caramel pecan sundae waffle. It will make you remember Hollywood with fondness.

OPPOSITE ABOVE The retro exterior of the Cinerama Dome at the ArcLight Cinema complex, built in 1963.

OPPOSITE BELOW A tour bus at the Walk of Fame.

ABOVE Roscoe's House of Chicken and Waffles keeps its soul-food promise: gravy and waffles come with the chicken.

THE BASICS

Fly into Los Angeles, Long Beach, Ontario, or Burbank. For touring, you can get by without a car.

The Hollywood Roosevelt
7000 Hollywood Boulevard
800-950-7667
hollywoodroosevelt.com
$$$
Can be loud, but historic as a favorite of stars in Hollywood's early days. All the night life you'll ever want.

Hollywood Hills Hotel
1999 North Sycamore Avenue
323-850-1909
hollywoodhillshotel.com
$$
A hillside landmark, and a bargain.

The Redbury @ Hollywood and Vine
1717 Vine Street
323-962-1717
theredbury.com
$$$-$$$$
Chic new boutique hotel at a famous corner.

Pasadena

Nestled in the San Gabriel Valley just 10 miles northeast of Los Angeles, Pasadena harbors a distinct, if at times chauvinistic, sense of individual self. Its old-money past continues to flourish in the form of grand mansions and a vast array of museums and gardens, many underwritten by prominent local families. And newer money has helped transform Old Pasadena, in decline for many years, into an energetic shopping and dining destination, with quirky shops and new restaurants. But it is the expansive outdoors, mountain views, and fine climate (except in August, when you could fry a hot dog at the Rose Bowl) that still make Pasadena, the famed City of Roses, a shining jewel of Southern California and an enduring object of jealousy. — BY JENNIFER STEINHAUER

FRIDAY

1 *Dream House* 3 p.m.

Real estate can go boom or bust, but either way envy is epidemic in Pasadena, and few homes are more desirable than the **Gamble House** (4 Westmoreland Place; 626-793-3334; gamblehouse.org). While the tour guides can reinforce a certain preciousness, there is no denying the allure of this Craftsman-style home, built in 1908 for David and Mary Gamble of the Procter & Gamble Company by the architects Charles Sumner Greene and Henry Mather Greene. To protect the floors, flat shoes are required for the hourlong tour. But they'll give you a pair of slippers if you're wearing your Jimmy Choos.

2 *Rose Bowl* 4:30 p.m.

Well, you're here, so why not see where it all happens each winter? You can tool around the Rose Bowl grounds, jog, enjoy the gardens, and imagine you are a rose queen — or one of the many whose efforts add up to the 80,000 hours needed to put together the **Tournament of Roses** (391 South Orange Grove Boulevard; 626-449-4100; tournamentofroses.com).

3 *Burritoville* 6:30 p.m.

There's a depressing number of fast-food restaurants in town, serving the same grub found in any American mall. But one standout is **El Toreo Cafe** (21 South Fair Oaks Avenue; 626-793-2577; $), a hole-in-the-wall that serves terrific and inexpensive

Mexican food. Try the carnitas burritos and chile verde, with large helpings and authentic flair.

4 *Retail Hop* 8:30 p.m.

Many stores in Old Pasadena stay open late. Skip the chains-o-plenty and make your way down Colorado Boulevard, the central corridor, and its side streets. Among the finds: **Distant Lands Travel Bookstore and Outfitters** (20 South Raymond Avenue; 626-449-3220; distantlands.com), which sells travel paraphernalia like Africa maps and packing kits; **Elisa B.** (16 East Holly Street; 626-397-4770; elisab.com), where the sales staff will get you out of your mom jeans; and **Lula Mae** (100 North Fair Oaks Avenue; 626-304-9996; lulamae.com) for candles and weird gifts like bride-and-groom maracas. End the evening by having some peanut butter or malaga gelato at **Tutti Gelati** (62 West Union Street; 626-440-9800).

SATURDAY

5 *Morning Sweets* 9 a.m.

All good vacation days begin with hot chocolate, so follow the California Institute of Technology

OPPOSITE The Japanese garden at the Huntington Library, Art Collections, and Botanical Gardens.

BELOW Changing shoes outside the Rose Bowl.

students to **Euro Pane** (950 East Colorado Boulevard; 626-577-1828) and order a hot cup of the chocolaty goodness, along with fresh breads and flaky croissants, which are first-rate. A counter filled with children's books helps keep the young ones entertained.

6 *Fun Under the Sun* 10 a.m.

While children's museums often induce an instant throbbing in the temple — and an urge to reach for a hand sanitizer — a happy exception is **Kidspace Children's Museum** (480 North Arroyo Boulevard; 626-449-9144; kidspacemuseum.org), an active museum where adults can chill with a book under the sun while the kids ride tricycles, check out the dig site, and climb around the mini-model of the city's Arroyo Seco canyon, where it actually "rains" from time to time. The Splash Dance Fountain is a winner.

7 *Order the Obvious* 1 p.m.

No day in Pasadena should pass without a stop at **Pie 'n Burger** (913 East California Boulevard; 626-795-1123; pienburger.com; $), a local institution since 1963. Go ahead and have a chicken pot pie, which is beyond decent, or some pancakes if you're feeling all vegan about it, but honestly, the burger is the way to go. It is a juicy concoction served up in old-school paper liners, with the requisite Thousand Island dressing on the bun. Finish the whole thing

off with a sublime slice of banana cream or cherry pie. Just don't tarry — there are bound to be large groups of folks waiting to get their hands on burgers, too.

8 *Master Class* 3 p.m.

Even if you're feeling a bit tired, there is something oddly relaxing about the **Norton Simon Museum of Art** (411 West Colorado Boulevard; 626-449-6840; nortonsimon.org). There's Degas's *Little Dancer Aged 14*, Van Gogh's *Portrait of a Peasant*, Diego Rivera's *The Flower Vendor*. Natural light streams in from skylights, and a sensible layout makes this a pleasant place to while away the afternoon — not to mention examining the star collection of Western paintings and sculpture from the 14th to 20th centuries. Don't skip the South Asian art downstairs, especially the Buddha Shakyamuni, which sits majestically outdoors. The guided audio tours are quite good.

9 *Solid Italian* 7 p.m.

After a day of cultural and sun soaking, nestle into **Gale's Restaurant** (452 South Fair Oaks Avenue; 626-432-6705; galesrestaurant.com; $$$). A totally local spot, it offers remarkably solid fare just down the road from all the hubbub. Couples, families, and friends who seem to have just finished a day outdoors snuggle amid the brick walls and small wooden tables, drinking wine from slightly cheesy Brighton goblets. Start it off with some warm roasted olives or a steamed artichoke and then move on to the country-style Tuscan steak or caprese salad. For dessert skip the leaden cheesecake and go instead for the poppy seed cake, which is uncommonly tasty.

SUNDAY

10 *Garden Party* 10:30 a.m.

An entire day barely covers a corner of the **Huntington Library, Art Collections, and Botanical Gardens** (1151 Oxford Road, San Marino; 626-405-2100; huntington.org). There are 120 acres of gardens, an enormous library of rare manuscripts and books,

and three permanent art galleries featuring British and French artists of the 18th and 19th centuries. Here is a good plan for a morning: Take a quick run through the exhibit of American silver. Ooh and ahh. Then pick one of the gardens to tour. The Desert garden, with its bizarre-looking cactuses and lunarlike landscapes, is a winner, though the Japanese and Jungle gardens are close rivals. Top it off at the Children's garden, where interactive exhibits can get kids dirty, which pleases everyone but the one stuck changing all the wet shirts. Stay for tea; there's no dress code in the tea room.

OPPOSITE The Gamble House, designed by Charles Sumner Greene and Henry Mather Greene for members of a founding family of Procter & Gamble.

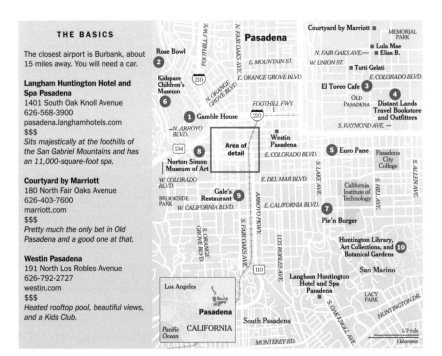

THE BASICS

The closest airport is Burbank, about 15 miles away. You will need a car.

Langham Huntington Hotel and Spa Pasadena
1401 South Oak Knoll Avenue
626-568-3900
pasadena.langhamhotels.com
$$$
Sits majestically at the foothills of the San Gabriel Mountains and has an 11,000-square-foot spa.

Courtyard by Marriott
180 North Fair Oaks Avenue
626-403-7600
marriott.com
$$$
Pretty much the only bet in Old Pasadena and a good one at that.

Westin Pasadena
191 North Los Robles Avenue
626-792-2727
westin.com
$$$
Heated rooftop pool, beautiful views, and a Kids Club.

(Map of Pasadena and San Marino area, showing: Rose Bowl, Kidspace Children's Museum, Gamble House, Norton Simon Museum of Art, Gale's Restaurant, Brookside Park, Westin Pasadena, El Toreo Cafe, Old Pasadena, Distant Lands Travel Bookstore and Outfitters, Euro Pane, Pasadena City College, California Institute of Technology, Pie'n Burger, Courtyard by Marriott, Lula Mae, Elisa B., Tutti Gelati, Huntington Library, Art Collections, and Botanical Gardens, San Marino, Langham Huntington Hotel and Spa Pasadena, Lacy Park, Memorial Park, Los Angeles, South Pasadena. Inset: California, Pacific Ocean, Pasadena. Scale: 1/2 mile, 1 kilometer)

Santa Monica

When Angelenos think of the perfect beach town, they think of Santa Monica. With its classic amusement pier, glittering bay, and surfers bobbing on swells, it certainly looks the part. But take a short walk inland, and there's a town asserting its unique identity: eight square miles and about 100,000 people surrounded by districts of the City of Los Angeles, but stubbornly remaining a separate city. A well-preserved Mission-style bungalow sits around the corner from a steel performance space by Frank Gehry. Shops sell goods ranging from vintage Parisian wedding gowns to a whimsical map made entirely of license plates. Enjoy the games and famed carousel of the Santa Monica Pier, and then step back from the beach to sample the city's variety the way Santa Monicans do.
— BY FRED A. BERNSTEIN AND LOUISE TUTELIAN

FRIDAY

1 *Landscape and Seascape* 4 p.m.

James Corner, an architect of the High Line park in Manhattan, has transformed a former parking lot into **Tongva Park** (tongvapark.squarespace.com), a stunning 6.2-acre space with sculptural art, fountains, play areas, and winding walkways. Take a walk there, and then, for a sense of the setting that made Santa Monica, stroll in **Palisades Park** (Ocean Avenue at Santa Monica Boulevard; smgov.net/parks) and wander off on one of the sinuous paths overlooking the beach and Santa Monica Pier.

2 *Oyster Shack* 6 p.m.

The **Blue Plate Oysterette** (1355 Ocean Avenue; 310-576-3474; blueplatesantamonica.com; $$), one of the dozen or so Santa Monica restaurants that face the ocean, may be the most ocean-y, with its raw bar and daily specials like pan-seared rainbow trout. The casual blue-and-white restaurant, with a tin-pressed ceiling and blackboard menus, draws a chic, flip-flop-wearing crowd.

3 *The View That Moves* 8 p.m.

At sunset, the most thrilling view in town is at the beach, from the top of the solar-powered, 130-foot-high Pacific Wheel, the Ferris wheel at the **Santa Monica Pier**. Yes, it's touristy, and yes, it

might be crowded, but it is, after all, the city's iconic symbol. As you glide upward, watching the entire city of Santa Monica, and far beyond, slide into view, the whole scene will be bathed in the sunset-colored glow. If you prefer a view that's not mobile, head south into Venice to the rooftop lounge of the **Hotel Erwin** (1697 Pacific Avenue; 310-452-1111; hotelerwin.com), where the banquettes seem to hang over the beach. Gaze at a Santa Monica panorama while sipping a cocktail. You can reserve a table in advance through the hotel's website.

SATURDAY

4 *Duck for Breakfast* 8 a.m.

The lines spill out the door, so arrive early at **Huckleberry Bakery and Café** (1014 Wilshire Boulevard; 310-451-2311; huckleberrycafe.com; $$). Breakfast favorites include green eggs and ham, made with pesto and prosciutto, and duck hash with sunny-side-up eggs. The cheerful room, with wooden tables and colorful accents, feels like a large country bakery.

5 *Into the Mountains* 9 a.m.

The Backbone Trail, a 69-mile system, roughly follows the crest of the Santa Monica Mountains north

OPPOSITE Palisades Park, overlooking the Pacific Ocean.

BELOW The Isaac Milbank House, designed by the firm that did Grauman's Chinese Theater, is one of the Craftsman-style houses on Adelaide Drive designated as city landmarks.

from **Will Rogers State Historic Park** just north of Santa Monica (1501 Will Rogers State Park Road, off West Sunset Boulevard, Pacific Palisades; 310-454-8212; nps.gov/samo/planyourvisit/backbonetrail.htm). Hikers can take an easy, sage-scented, two-mile loop from the parking lot at Will Rogers up to Inspiration Point, a sensational overlook of Santa Monica Bay from the Palos Verdes Peninsula to Point Dume in Malibu. Do it on a clear day, and you'll see Catalina Island and the white dots of sails. Behind are the slopes of the Santa Monica Mountains, and in the distance, the high-rises of downtown Los Angeles. Up here, the muted chattering of birds and the hum of insects are the only sounds.

6 *Builders and Shoppers* Noon

Back in northern Santa Monica, natural sights give way to architectural ones. Two houses designated as city landmarks are the Craftsman-style **Isaac Milbank House** (236 Adelaide Drive) — designed by the same firm that did Grauman's Chinese Theater in Hollywood — and the stucco **Worrel House** (710 Adelaide Drive), which was built in the mid-1920s and has been described as a "Pueblo-Revival Maya fantasy." Some of the city's best shopping is nearby on Montana Avenue. It's all one-of-a-kind at **Marcia Bloom Designs** (1527 Montana Avenue; 310-393-0985; marciabloomdesigns.com), a gallery/boutique with whimsical gypsy-like skirts, casual Southwestern styles, and statement tops, scarves, gloves, bags, and caps — all of it crafted by the artist-owner herself. **Rooms & Gardens** (No. 1311-A; 310-451-5154; roomsandgardens.com) sells furniture, antiques, and accessories like pillows fashioned from antique Indian saris.

7 *Art Lovers, Art Buyers* 3 p.m.

For an art-filled afternoon, start at **Bergamot Station** (2525 Michigan Avenue; 310-453-7535; bergamotstation.com), built on the site of a former trolley-line stop. The highlight of this complex of art galleries is the **Santa Monica Museum of Art**

(310-586-6488; smmoa.org). Off the 3rd Street Promenade, find the unconventional **Adamm's Stained Glass Studio & Art Gallery** (1426 4th Street; 310-451-9390; adammsgallery.com), an interesting spot that even locals often overlook. The work of more than 175 glass artists is for sale, from gemlike paperweights to frilly perfume bottles and sculptural chandeliers.

8 *Bistro Evenings* 8 p.m.

There are lots of stylish hotels in Santa Monica, and some of them offer very good food. A case in point is **Fig** (101 Wilshire Boulevard; 310-319-3111; figsantamonica.com; $$$), a contemporary American bistro at the Fairmont Miramar Hotel. The menu features seasonal ingredients and dishes like a halibut "chop" or snap peas with mint. There is seating indoors, in an elegant room with starburst mirrors, as well as on the terrace with views of the ocean through the lush gardens. The huge Moreton Bay fig tree, from which the restaurant gets its name, will make you feel like climbing.

9 *Disco Nights* 11 p.m.

Santa Monica may be known for sunshine, but there's plenty to do after dark. For a taste of the local night life, head to **Zanzibar** (1301 Fifth Street; 310-451-2221; zanzibarlive.com), a cavernous club that manages to be both cozy and contemporary. It is also the rare venue that seems able to please young and old — you could imagine Joni Mitchell on the dance floor with her grandkids. The D.J.'s play a mix of hip-hop, R&B, and top 40. Even the décor has crossover appeal; hanging from the ceiling are perforated copper lanterns (for a vaguely African feeling) and disco balls.

10 *No Wet Suit Needed* 10 a.m.

Even in warm weather, the waters of Southern California can be frigid. For a more comfortable swim, duck into the **Annenberg Community Beach House** (415 Pacific Coast Highway; 310-458-4904; annenbergbeachhouse.com), a sleek public facility that opened in 2010. The pool is spectacular, and you can buy a day pass for a reasonable price. If

you've got to get in your laps after October, your best bet is the public **Santa Monica Swim Center** (2225 16th Street; 310-458-8700; smgov.net/aquatics), where the adult and children's pools are kept at 79 and 85 degrees, respectively.

11 *Sunday Retail* Noon

Amid the sneaker stores and used book shops of artsy Main Street, in the Ocean Park neighborhood, look for the Frank Gehry-designed steel boxes of **Edgemar** (2415-2449 Main Street; edgemarcenter.org), which house retail tenants and a performance space around an open courtyard. Gehry's retail footprint in Santa Monica has shrunk since his **Santa Monica Place**, designed in 1980, was replaced by a new version (395 Santa Monica Place; santamonicaplace.com), a glassy open-air retail

complex that often has live music, HDTV displays, or seasonal events. If shopping makes you hungry, head for the top level and the **Curious Palate** market, which has a cafe with an artisanal, farm-to-table menu.

OPPOSITE Ocean-view dining at Santa Monica Place, a glassy new open-air version of a California shopping mall.

ABOVE At sunset, the best view in town is at the beach, from the top of the solar-powered, 130-foot-high Pacific Wheel, the Ferris wheel at the Santa Monica Pier.

THE BASICS

Santa Monica is about a 20-minute drive from Los Angeles International Airport. There's a terrific bus system (bigbluebus.com), but most visitors find it more convenient to drive.

The Ambrose
1255 20th Street
310-315-1555
ambrosehotel.com
$$$
Feels like a Mission-style hideaway with stained-glass windows.

Hotel Shangri-La
1301 Ocean Avenue
310-394-2791
shangrila-hotel.com
$$$$
A storied, bright-white apparition on bluffs high above the Pacific.

Shore Hotel
1515 Ocean Avenue
310-458-1515
shorehotel.com
$$$$
Across Ocean Avenue from the pier.

Malibu

Locals call it "the Bu" — a laid-back, celebrity-filled strip of a city that sparkles in the collective consciousness as a sun-drenched state of mind. With the busy Pacific Coast Highway running through and no discernible center of town, some of the best of Malibu, which has around 13,000 residents, can disappear in a drive-by. The staggering natural beauty of the sea and mountains is obvious, but pull off the road and stay awhile, and you'll find more: a world-class art museum, local wines, top-notch restaurants, and chic shops.
— BY LOUISE TUTELIAN

FRIDAY

1 *The Wind, the Waves...* 5 p.m.

What's so appealing about Malibu's little slice of coast? Visit **Point Dume State Preserve** (Birdview Avenue and Cliffside Drive; 310-457-8143; parks.ca.gov), and you'll see. A modest walk to the top of this coastal bluff rewards you with a sweeping view of the entire Santa Monica Bay, the inland Santa Monica Mountains, and, on a clear day, Catalina Island. A boardwalk just below the summit leads to a platform for watching swooping pelicans and crashing waves. To feel the sand between your toes, drive down Birdview Avenue to Westward Beach Road and park at the very end of the lot on your left. You'll be looking at Westward Beach, a gem that most visitors miss. Strike a yoga pose. Sigh at will.

2 *Chasing the Sunset* 7 p.m.

Little known fact: Most of Malibu faces south, not west. That means sitting down at just any seaside restaurant at dusk won't guarantee seeing a sunset over the water. But the aptly named **Sunset Restaurant** (6800 Westward Beach Road; 310-589-1007; thesunsetrestaurant.com) is a sure bet, with just the right orientation. Claim a white leather banquette, order a carafe of wine and select a tasting plate of cheeses, and settle in for the light show.

3 *Shore Dinner* 9 p.m.

If you're going to spot a celebrity, chances are it will be at **Nobu Malibu** (3835 Cross Creek Road, in the Malibu Country Mart; 310-317-9140; nobumatsuhisa.com; $$$), one of the famed chef Nobu Matsuhisa's many restaurants. The sushi

is sublime, and the entrees measure up. Reservations are essential. The front room is convivial but noisy; the subtly lighted back room is quieter.

SATURDAY

4 *Walk the Pier* 9 a.m.

The 780-foot-long **Malibu Pier** (23000 Pacific Coast Highway; 888-310-7437; malibupiersportfishing.com) is the most recognizable (and, arguably, only) landmark in town. Take a morning stroll out to the end, chat with the fishermen, and watch surfers paddle out. You'll be walking on a piece of Malibu history. The pier was originally built in 1905 as a loading dock for construction material, and it was a lookout during World War II. It crops up in numerous movies and TV shows.

5 *Bronze for the Ages* 10 a.m.

The **Getty Villa** (17985 Pacific Coast Highway; 310-440-7300; getty.edu) is just over the city's southern border in Pacific Palisades, but no matter: it shouldn't be missed. The museum, built by J. Paul Getty in the 1970s to resemble a first-century Roman country house, contains Greek, Roman, and Etruscan vessels, gems, and statuary, some dating back to 6500 B.C. On the second floor is a rare life-size Greek bronze, *Statue of a Victorious Youth*, a prize of the

OPPOSITE Beach and pier at Malibu, the little slice of Pacific coast that celebrities like to call their own.

BELOW Kai Sanson, a surfing instructor, initiates students into the ways of the waves.

museum. In the outside peristyle gardens, watch the sun glint off bronze statues at the 220-foot-long reflecting pool. Admission is free, but parking is limited, so car reservations are required.

6 *Magic Carpet Tile* 1 p.m.

Even many longtime Angelenos don't know about the **Adamson House** (23200 Pacific Coast Highway; 310-456-9575; adamsonhouse.org), a 1930 Spanish Colonial Revival residence that's a showplace of exquisite ceramic tile from Malibu Potteries, which closed in 1932. Overlooking Surfrider Beach with a view of Malibu Pier, the house belonged to a member of the Rindge family, the last owners of the Malibu Spanish land grant. Take a tour and watch for the Persian "carpet" constructed entirely from intricately patterned pieces of tile. Other highlights: a stunning star-shaped fountain and a bathroom tiled top to bottom in an ocean pattern, with ceramic galleons poised in perpetuity on pointy whitecaps in a sea of blue.

7 *Vino With a View* 4 p.m.

The drive to **Malibu Family Wines** (31740 Mulholland Highway; 818-865-0605; malibuwines.com) along the serpentine roads of the Santa Monica Mountains is almost as much fun as tipping a glass once you get there. Set on a serene green lawn, the tasting room is really a covered outdoor stone and wood counter. Sidle up and choose a flight of four styles. Or buy a bottle and lounge at one of the tables. (Tip: Regulars request the horseshoes or bocce ball set at the counter.) And don't miss the collection of vintage pickup trucks spread around the property.

8 *Can You Say Olé?* 7 p.m.

Located in the chic **Malibu Lumber Yard** shopping arcade (the piles of two-by-fours are long gone) you'll find **Café Habana Malibu** (3939 Cross Creek Road; 310-317-0300; habana-malibu.com), the West Coast hermana of famed Café Habana in the West Village in New York and Habana Outpost in Brooklyn. The sleek, solar-powered bar and café

serves Mexican/Cuban fare from 11 a.m. to — most nights — an unheard-of 1 a.m. in early-to-bed L.A. (There's Wednesday karaoke and a nightclub vibe after dark.) Locals tout the fish tacos and charred cheese-covered corn on the cob, and the killer margaritas and mojitos. Yes, the guacamole is the price of a diner entree, but the star-sightings are free.

SUNDAY

9 *Ride the Surf* 10 a.m.

Surf shops offering lessons and board rentals line the Pacific Coast Highway (P.C.H. in local lingo), but Kai Sanson of **Zuma Surf and Swim Training** (949-742-1086; zumasurfandswim.com) takes his fun seriously. Sanson, a Malibu native, will size you up with a glance and gear the instruction to your skills. There's a price for the lessons, but his tales of growing up in Malibu are free. Locals also give high marks to **Malibu Makos Surf Club** (310-317-1229; malibumakos.com).

10 *Brunch in Style* Noon

Put on your oversize sunglasses if you're going to **Geoffrey's Malibu** (27400 Pacific Coast Highway; 310-457-1519; geoffreysmalibu.com; $$$). Geoffrey's (pronounced Joffreys) is the hot meeting spot for

ABOVE The curve of the Pacific beach in Malibu. The houses lining the waterside are worth millions.

BELOW Tasting the reds at Malibu Family Wines.

the well-heeled with a hankering for a shiitake mushroom omelet or lobster Cobb salad. Its Richard Neutra-designed building overlooks the Pacific, and every table has an ocean view. Or if you want something a bit more chill, head to **Ollo** (23750 Pacific Coast Highway in the Malibu Colony Plaza; 310-317-1444; ollomalibu.com; $$) and load up on the generous — and locally sourced — pancakes, huevos rancheros, etc., while lounging in the dining room or sunning on the patio in the ocean breeze.

11 *Shop Like a Star* 2 p.m.

Whether it's diamonds or designer jeans you're after, the open-air **Malibu Country Mart** (3835 Cross Creek Road; malibucountrymart.com) is the place

to cruise for them. Its more than 50 retail stores and restaurants include Ralph Lauren, 7 for All Mankind, and John Varvatos. In an adjacent space is the luxe **Malibu Lumber Yard** shopping complex (themalibulumberyard.com), with stores like Alice + Olivia and AllSaints Spitalfields.

ABOVE The Getty Villa museum, built by J. Paul Getty to resemble a first-century Roman country house.

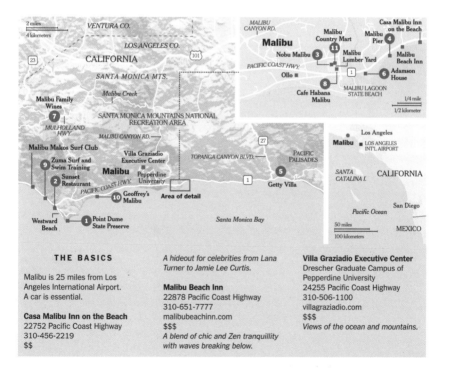

THE BASICS

Malibu is 25 miles from Los Angeles International Airport. A car is essential.

Casa Malibu Inn on the Beach
22752 Pacific Coast Highway
310-456-2219
$$

A hideout for celebrities from Lana Turner to Jamie Lee Curtis.

Malibu Beach Inn
22878 Pacific Coast Highway
310-651-7777
malibubeachinn.com
$$$
A blend of chic and Zen tranquillity with waves breaking below.

Villa Graziadio Executive Center
Drescher Graduate Campus of Pepperdine University
24255 Pacific Coast Highway
310-506-1100
villagraziadio.com
$$$
Views of the ocean and mountains.

Long Beach

At the mouth of the Los Angeles River in Long Beach, California, shipping cranes flex their silhouettes across the skyline — an industrial panorama that suits the city's role as one of the world's busiest ports. But while its maritime character remains, Long Beach has shed much of its grittiness and now welcomes cruise ships as well as cargo vessels. Along with its 11 miles of beaches, it has a compact downtown of low-rising Art Deco towers, unassuming neighborhoods where Craftsman bungalows are ringed by tropical gardens, excellent museums, and a tangle of Southern California subcultures. Layered, urban, and unexpected, it is a city apart from the sprawl and strip malls that define the outer edges of Los Angeles. — BY FREDA MOON

FRIDAY

1 *Ship Shape* 3:30 p.m.
Coming across today as equal parts kitsch and Streamline Moderne grandeur, the *Queen Mary* (1126 Queens Highway; 877-342-0742; queenmary.com), which first crossed the Atlantic in 1936, is now permanently docked in Long Beach Harbor, where it serves as a 1,019-foot, 12-deck floating hotel and museum. Walk the worn teak decks and peer into the sumptuous staterooms, and it takes only a small mental leap to feel as if you're making an Atlantic crossing alongside Clark Gable and Marlene Dietrich. For a cocktail or glass of house bubbly, stop in the ship's grand dining room, **Sir Winston's**, at sunset. The harbor area also calls out to tourists with a giant Ferris wheel and the **Aquarium of the Pacific** (100 Aquarium Way; 562-590-3100; aquariumofpacific.org), which displays thousands of fish and marine animals.

2 *Sustainable Supper* 8 p.m.
Technically in Signal Hill, a small, incorporated city surrounded by Long Beach, **Delius Restaurant** (2951 Cherry Avenue, Signal Hill; 562-426-0694; deliusrestaurant.com; $$) is four miles from downtown, on an avenue dominated by car dealerships. But in a city with more taco trucks and neon-clad diners than sophisticated restaurants, Delius is worth the trip. The seven-course prix fixe menu changes monthly, and the à la carte menu includes regional renditions of New American staples; for example,

an appetizer of duck confit with teardrop tomatoes, tomato yogurt spheres, upland cress, queso fresco, and mole.

SATURDAY

3 *Ethnic Explorations* 9 a.m.
To begin a morning celebrating Long Beach multiculturalism, start with breakfast at **Kafe Neo** (2800 East Fourth Street; 562-987-1210; kafeneolb.com; $$), which serves Hellenic standards like kayana (an omelet with tomato and feta, topped with house-made marinara) and loukaniko sausage, along with almond-crusted French toast. From there, it's a short drive to the **Museum of Latin American Art** (628 Alamitos Avenue; 562-437-1689; molaa.org), which has one of the largest collections of contemporary Latin American paintings and sculpture anywhere. Make another stop at the small **Pacific Island Ethnic Art Museum** (695 Alamitos Avenue; 562-216-4170; pieam.org), which has a brilliantly hued mural of a traditional Micronesian A-frame, with exhibits that include sculptures, textiles, paintings, and jewelry from across Oceania.

4 *California Classic* 1 p.m.
Pull up a plastic patio chair at **Steamed** (801 East Third Street; 562-437-1122; steamedcuisine.com; $$)

OPPOSITE Long Beach, seen from the *Queen Mary*.

BELOW Shopping for vinyl records at Fingerprints.

for a quintessentially Southern California vegetarian lunch. It's in a converted bungalow, with terra-cotta tiled floors and Tibetan prayer flags, in the emerging East Village Arts District. Quesadillas and California-style burritos are exceptionally well prepared and are served with three kinds of house-made salsa and guacamole.

5 *Positively Fourth Street* 2 p.m.

After an elegant renovation, a former 1920s-era furniture store has become the cultural heart of the East Village district. An 8,000-square-foot building with exposed beams and original wood floors, it is now the home of **Fingerprints** (420 East Fourth Street; 562-433-4996; fingerprintsmusic.com), one of the Los Angeles area's last great record shops. Check the store calendar for coming appearances; longtime recording stars sometimes do signings. For a different kind of browsing, walk along Fourth Street's **Retro Row**, a stretch of second-hand boutiques and high-end antiques shops. You'll find a good selection of vintage clothes and store-brand clothes, furniture, and oddities like discontinued board games and faded erotica.

6 *Cambodian Repast* 7 p.m.

Long Beach is home to the largest Khmer community outside Cambodia. For Cambodian specialties, try the cavernous **Siem Reap Asian Cuisine** (1810 East Anaheim Street; 562-591-7414; siemreapkhmercuisine.

com; $), a dining hall with a bar, a small dance floor, and gaudy décor of plastic plants and wood carvings. The expansive menu features dishes like amok (fish cooked in young coconut) and banh chiao (ground chicken and bean sprout crepe).

7 *For Beer Lovers* 8:30 p.m.

If you like gastropubs, take a walk on downtown's promenade to check out **Beachwood BBQ and Brewing** (210 East Third Street; 562-436-4020; beachwoodbbq.com), where you can sit at the long counter and watch steam rising from stainless steel brew house tanks, or the cheerily sacrilegious **Congregation Ale House** (201 East Broadway; 562-432-2337; congregationalehouse.com), which has an inventory of over 100 craft beers.

8 *Jazz and Waffle* 10:30 p.m.

Roscoe's House of Chicken and Waffles — part of a chain of 24-hour soul food restaurants — may seem an odd choice for live music. But on Saturday nights, the **Seabird Jazz Lounge** at the Roscoe's in Long Beach (730 East Broadway; 562-522-8488; seabirdjazzloungelbc.com) draws fans for live performances. Another good spot for listening is **4th Street Vine** (2142 East Fourth Street; 562-343-5463; 4thstreetvine.com), a neighborhood wine bar with local art on the walls and blues or jazz bands on many weekend nights.

SUNDAY

9 *Mexican Morning* 9:30 a.m.

Expect a wait at the **Coffee Cup Cafe** (3734 East Fourth Street; 562-433-3292; coffeecupcafe-lb.com; $), a coffee shop with orange vinyl booths and unexpected touches, like modern art and spicy Mexican influences on an otherwise traditional diner menu. Try Hank's chicken chile verde omelet or the housemade apple honey sausage and eggs. For the kids, there are short stacks of banana nut or blueberry pancakes. You'll see why people line up.

10 *Afloat* 11 a.m.

The Naples neighborhood, concocted by a real estate developer in the 1920s, is an inviting complex of islands, streets, and canals, with Italianate design touches, reminiscent of the Venice neighborhood about 25 miles to the north in Los Angeles. Since 1983, couples yearning for romance have been able to rent an authentic Venetian gondola, complete with stripe-shirted gondolier, for an hourlong glide through its waterways (**Gondola Getaway**, 5437 East Ocean Boulevard; 562-433-9595; gondolagetawayinc.com). The ride might include a running commentary on the sights or a Verdi aria. For a more active alternative, go hydrobiking (**Long Beach Hydro Bikes**, 110 North Marina Drive; 562-546-2493; lbhydrobikes.com) in Alamitos Bay. A contemporary take on the sit-down paddle boat, hydrobikes are pedal-powered boats. Some can accommodate two people and a dog.

OPPOSITE Pleasure craft in the Long Beach Harbor.

THE BASICS

The Long Beach airport, an Art Deco relic from the days of pioneer aviators, pops up often in movies and is served now by several carriers. You will need a car.

Hotel Maya
700 Queensway Drive
562-435-7676
hotelmayalongbeach.com
$$
Spread across 11 waterfront acres.

Dockside Boat & Bed
Dock 5; Rainbow Harbor
562-436-3111
boatandbed.com
$$
Six luxury yachts, including a gorgeous 54-foot Stephens motor model, converted into a B & B.

The Varden
335 Pacific Avenue
562-432-8950
thevardenhotel.com
$$
Boutique hotel downtown.

Map labels

East Village Arts District
Fingerprints
Delius Restaurant — 2
Los Angeles
5 miles
2.5 kilometers
10
5
CALIFORNIA
405
Long Beach
Beachwood BBQ and Brewing — 5
W. FOURTH ST.
The Varden — 7
E. THIRD ST.
Signal Hill
405
W. BROADWAY
Congregation Ale House
ELM AVE.
CHERRY AVE.
E. OCEAN BLVD.
Long Beach
Pacific Ocean
San Pedro Bay
Los Angeles River
Pacific Island Ethnic Art Museum
ALAMITOS AVE.
Siem Reap Asian Cuisine — 6
E. ANAHEIM ST.
E. PACIFIC COAST HWY.
Museum of Latin American Art
Steamed — 4
E. SEVENTH ST.
E. FOURTH ST.
1
8
Coffee Cup Cafe — 9
Aquarium of the Pacific
Dockside Boat & Bed
Roscoe's House of Chicken and Waffles / Seabird Jazz Lounge
Gondola Getaway — 10
Hotel Maya
QUEENSWAY DR.
E. OCEAN BLVD.
Retro Row
4th Street Vine
E. SEVENTH ST.
Queen Mary / Sir Winston's — 1
ST. LOUIS AVE.
E. FOURTH ST.
Kafe Neo — 3
E. THIRD ST.
Long Beach Hydro Bikes
1 mile
2 kilometers

San Diego

Like its urban rival Los Angeles, San Diego is not so much a city as a loose collection of overlapping (and sometimes colliding) communities bound by arterial, life-giving freeways. It's a military town in Coronado; a surf town in funky, eclectic Ocean Beach; and a border town in the historic Mexican-American neighborhood of Barrio Logan. If San Diego has a cohesive identity at all, it's a shared embrace of an easy, breezy Southern California casualness. With its lack of pretension, the city is often seen by outsiders as a kind of Pleasantville — a bland, happy place with an exceptional amount of sunshine. Depending on how deep you look, that may be all you see. But there are, after all, worse things than Spanish tiles, palm trees, tropical blooms, year-round flip-flops, fresh fish tacos, and bonfires on the beach. — BY FREDA MOON

FRIDAY

1 *View Across the Bay* 4:30 p.m.

Sitting above the water on a stilted deck on Harbor Island, **C Level** (880 Harbor Island Drive; 619-298-6802; cohnrestaurants.com/islandprime) looks across San Diego Bay to the Naval ships at Coronado, downtown's towering skyline, and the tall ships at the Maritime Museum. Have a cool drink and enjoy snacks like rice-paper-wrapped prawns and steamed mussels with chorizo. Afterward, take a giddy ride on the Giant Dipper wooden roller coaster at Belmont Park (belmontpark.com), a vintage amusement park on the beach in Mission Bay.

2 *Pork Shop* 7 p.m.

Carnitas' Snack Shack (2632 University Avenue; 619-294-7675; carnitassnackshack.com; $), a popular spot with local crowds, is a glorified taco stand serving pork-centric comfort food — including carnitas tacos with guacamole and salsa fresca, braised Duroc pork belly with a frisée, apple and radish salad, a steak sandwich on jalapeño and Cheddar cheese bread — from a takeout window in North Park. The

shack is a squat structure with outdoor tables and heat lamps around back and a giant sculpture of a metal pig adorning its roof.

3 *Just About Normal* 8:30 p.m.

For dessert, head for Adams Avenue and try the house-made Mexican chocolate or banana walnut ice cream at the mom-and-pop **Mariposa Ice Cream** (3450 Adams Avenue; 619-284-5197; mariposaicecream.com) or the exotic Mexican-style popsicles, called paletas, in flavors like lavender lemonade, salted caramel, and mango-chile at **Viva Pops** (3330 Adams Avenue; 619-795-1080; ilovevivapops.com). Both shops close at 9 p.m. on weekends. You're in the buzzing Normal Heights neighborhood, so do some more exploring. Stop in at **Lestat's Coffee House** (3343 Adams Avenue; 619-282-0437; lestats.com), and check the events calendar for the attached concert space, which hosts local music acts, comedy shows, and open mic nights.

4 *Old School, New Age* 10:30 p.m.

In South Park, rockabillies and old-timers take turns playing shuffleboard at **Hamilton's Tavern** (1521 30th Street; 619-238-5460; hamiltonstavern. com), which has a daunting 28 taps, two cask beer engines, and some 200 bottled beers, and claims to be the city's oldest alehouse. Or, instead, have an only-in-California experience at **Kava Lounge** (2812 Kettner Boulevard; 619-543-0933; kavalounge. com), a New Age bar, dance club, and arts space that promotes "future planetary night life" in the form of vegan cocktails, experimental dance music, and class

OPPOSITE AND RIGHT Eye catchers in a Navy Town: *Unconditional Surrender*, by Seward Johnson, and the decommissioned aircraft carrier *Midway*, now a museum, occupying space along the San Diego Embarcadero.

offerings that include "Ballet for Belly Dancers" in a nondescript building identifiable only by the Eye of Providence painted above its entrance.

SATURDAY

5 *To the Shore* 9 a.m.

Cruise up the coast to the **Cottage** in La Jolla (7702 Fay Avenue; 858-454-8409; cottagelajolla.com; $$), a would-be surf bungalow with an umbrella-canopied patio, which makes use of the Western bounty with dishes like lemon ricotta pancakes; polenta with tomato relish, kale pesto, goat cheese sauce, and chives; and soy chorizo hash with scrambled eggs, black beans, and queso fresco. After breakfast, continue north to the 2,000-acre **Torrey Pines State Natural Reserve** (12600 North Torrey Pines Road; 858-755-2063; torreypine.org), home to the torrey pine, one of the rarest species of pine in the world; sandstone cliffs shaped by the sea; and a lagoon that hosts migrating seabirds.

6 *Mission Viejo* Noon

Founded in 1769 as the first of California's 21 missions, the **Mission Basilica San Diego de Alcala** (10818 San Diego Mission Road; 619-281-8449; missionsandiego.com) has a bloody and politically complicated past. Today it is an exceptionally peaceful place — an active parish on a hillside carpeted with ice plants, with a Spanish-style garden at its center and a gift shop that sells Mexican folk art like milagros (religious charms) and Talavera pottery. For lunch, head north to the **Island Style Cafe** (5950 Santo Road; 858-541-7002; islandstylecafe.com; $), a home-style Hawaiian cafe with fabric orchids on the tables and tropical landscape prints on the walls. Try the Korean-style fried chicken thighs, served with

ABOVE The Pacific from Sunset Cliffs.

RIGHT You could ride, but walking is also a nice way to make your way down the central thoroughfare of Balboa Park.

classic sides like macaroni salad, and a glass of POG (passion-orange-guava juice).

7 *Easy Does It* 4 p.m.

Back downtown, stroll along the **Embarcadero**, a two-mile stretch of downtown waterfront where a gentle sea breeze will lull you into a zombie-like state in no time. You'll pass *Unconditional Surrender*, a giant sculptural rendering of Alfred Eisenstaedt's famous VJ Day photo of a sailor kissing a nurse. The decommissioned aircraft carrier *Midway* sits nearby and can be admired from Tuna Harbor Park, a shady nook next to the touristy but tasty **Fish Market** restaurant (750 North Harbor Drive; 619-232-3474; thefishmarket.com; $$).

8 *Sea and Sky* 7 p.m.

In the perennial debate over where to find San Diego's best fish tacos, the line at **Blue Water Seafood Market & Grill** (3667 India Street; 619-497-0914; bluewaterseafoodsandiego.com; $) is one indication. The menu reads like a choose-your-own aquatic adventure, listing a dozen kinds of seafood including Scottish salmon, Hawaiian albacore, and Alaskan halibut; six kinds of marinade (among them: chipotle, blackened, and "bronzed"); and four preparations: salad, sandwich, plate, or tacos. After you've eaten, have a nightcap next door at **Aero Club** (3365 India; 619-297-7211; aeroclubbar.com), a charmingly divey whiskey bar with some 600 bottles climbing the wall and toy airplanes hanging from the ceiling. Or eat a bit earlier and head up to Mission Hills to **Cinema Under the Stars** (4040 Goldfinch Street;

619-295-4221; topspresents.com), an open-air theater with zero-gravity lounge chairs, for an 8 p.m. movie.

SUNDAY

9 *Very Old California* 9 a.m.

Take a slow Sunday drive down the coast, past the sandstone Sunset Cliffs to the **Cabrillo National Monument** (1800 Cabrillo Memorial Drive; 619-557-5450; nps.gov/cabr). Walk the two-mile Bayside Trail along a rocky point of sage scrub and maguey plants, near where in 1542 Juan Rodriguez Cabrillo led the first European expedition to the coast of what is now California.

10 *Park and Ride* Noon

With 15 museums, one of the country's most-respected zoos, and 1,200 acres of hills, gardens,

forests, and ravines, **Balboa Park** (1549 El Prado; 619-239-0512; balboapark.org) cannot be fully explored in a weekend, much less an afternoon. But, for an overview, **San Diego Fly Rides** (1237 Prospect Street; 619-888-3878; sandiegoflyrides.com) uses high-end electric bikes, which can travel up to 20 m.p.h., to cover nine miles of ground on its two-hour Spanish Twist tour.

ABOVE Strolling the Embarcadero, a breezy two-mile stretch of waterfront. As the sculpture seems to suggest, fish is often on the menu at the restaurants nearby.

THE BASICS

Numerous airlines fly to San Diego. Or drive two hours from Los Angeles.

Hotel Indigo
San Diego-Gaslamp Quarter
509 Ninth Avenue
619-727-4000
hotelindigo.com
$$
A 3,800-square-foot green roof, free wireless, and a terrace bar.

Andaz San Diego
600 F Street
619-849-1234
sandiego.andaz.hyatt.com
$$$
Modern rooms, a four-story nightclub, and a flashy Philippe Starck-Katsuya Uechi restaurant.

Hotel del Coronado
1500 Orange Avenue
619-435-6611
hoteldel.com
$$$$
Beachside grande dame.

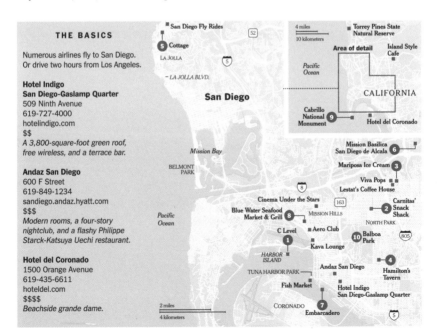

Palm Springs

Palm Springs was once the miles-from-Hollywood getaway that Malibu is now: a place for '60s movers and shakers to eat, drink, and sunbathe poolside while they awaited calls from studio execs. Today, after some hard-earned changes, this California desert town nestled in the Coachella Valley is becoming a destination for laid-back cool once again. The revival of modernism that inspired makeovers of its midcentury hotels, restaurants, and shops brought a revival of style, and the desert sun has never lost its appeal. Now Palm Springs attracts visitors who are just as happy climbing canyons as sipping cocktails on a lounge chair amid the design and architectural treasures of the past.
— BY ERICA CERULO

FRIDAY

1 *Cruising on Two Wheels* 3 p.m.

Because of its modest size, Palm Springs can easily become familiar over a couple of days, or even a few hours. Start your trip with a self-guided bike tour. **Big Wheel Tours** (760-779-1837; bwbtours.com) rents bicycles and can arrange bike and hiking tours. Free maps are available at the **Palm Springs Visitors Center** (2901 North Palm Canyon Drive; 760-778-8418; palm-springs.org). To scope out the dramatic terrain and local hot spots, pedal the Downtown Loop, which can be done in less than an hour, or the 10-mile Citywide Loop that takes you past the Moorten Botanical Gardens.

2 *Austria and Beyond* 7 p.m.

At **Johannes** (196 South Indian Canyon Drive; 760-778-0017; johannesrestaurants.com; $$$), the chef Johannes Bacher bills the food as modern Austrian, combining classic Central European specialties like spaetzle and sauerkraut with decidedly borrowed ingredients and flavors, ranging from polenta to wasabi. But one of the best dishes is also the most traditional: a heaping plate of Wiener schnitzel with parsley potatoes, cucumber salad, and cranberry compote.

3 *Partying Poolside* 9:30 p.m.

Back when Frank Sinatra held raucous shindigs at his Twin Palms home, Palm Springs was known for its party scene. These days, the best drinking establishments are in hotels. The white stucco exterior of the **Colony Palms Hotel** (572 North Indian Canyon Drive; 760-969-1800; colonypalmshotel.com) conceals a welcoming hideaway with stone walkways, towering palms, and, when needed, patio heaters. At the buzzing restaurant **Purple Palm**, ask to be seated by the pool and order a plate of Humboldt Fog chèvre, organic honey, and local dates with your drink to top off the night.

SATURDAY

4 *Modernist America* 9:30 a.m.

Along with the moneyed 20th-century tourists came eye-catching buildings: hotels, commercial spaces, and vacation homes. Next to a hopping Starbucks on the main drag sits one of the city's oldest architectural touchstones: a concrete bell tower salvaged from the long-gone Oasis Hotel, which was designed by Lloyd Wright (son of Frank) in 1924. This spot is also where Robert Imber, the often seersucker-clad architectural guru and one-man show behind **PS Modern Tours** (760-318-6118; palmspringsmoderntours.com), starts his three-hour excursions, which provide a survey of the city's key structures with a focus on the midcentury sweet

OPPOSITE Indian Canyons, a natural oasis on the Agua Caliente Indian Reservation just outside Palm Springs.

RIGHT The Kaufmann House, designed by Richard Neutra.

spot. Design enthusiasts can catch glimpses of the iconic Albert Frey-designed Tramway Gas Station, Richard Neutra's 1946 Kaufmann Desert House, and the mass-produced but stunning Alexander homes that your guide identifies by pointing out the four key components — "garage, breezeway, windows, wall" — in their various arrangements. Reserve well in advance.

5 Chic Cheek 1 p.m.

The wait for brunch at **Cheeky's** (622 North Palm Canyon Drive; 760-327-7595; cheekysps.com; $$) should be a tip-off: the bright, streamlined space, which feels airlifted from L.A. — in a good way — is popular. The standard eggs and waffles are spiced up with ingredients like beet relish, homemade herbed ricotta, and sour cherry compote.

6 Used Goods 3 p.m.

Stroll **Palm Canyon Drive**, a strip that's terrific for high-end vintage shopping, if a little dangerous for those who quickly reach for their credit cards. Among the many stores that focus on better-with-age décor, just a few have mastered the art of curating. At **a La MOD** (844 North Palm Canyon Drive; 760-327-0707; alamod768.com), nearly 70 percent of the merchandise, which is heavy on Lucite and lighting, is sourced locally, according to the shop's owners. Across the street, **Modern Way** (745 North Palm Canyon Drive; 760-320-5455; psmodernway.com) stocks an eclectic collection of larger pieces like Arthur Elrod couches, Verner Panton cone chairs, and Hans Olsen dining sets. For something you can actually take home, shop **Bon Vivant** (766 North Palm Canyon Drive, No. 3; 760-534-3197; gmcb.com), where the charming proprietors make you feel like a genuine collector for purchasing an $18 engraved brass vase or a $5 tie clip.

7 Stay Silly 5 p.m.

At the **Palm Springs Yacht Club**, at the **Parker Palm Springs** hotel (4200 East Palm Canyon Drive;

760-770-5000; theparkerpalmsprings.com/spa), standard spa offerings like deep-tissue rubdowns and wrinkle-fighting facials come with a playful attitude of retro irony. The pampering is real. Expect to pay high-end prices (some treatment packages are well over $300) but go away feeling refreshed and maybe — is it possible? — a little younger.

8 Friend of the House 8 p.m.

Most of the favored area restaurants have an old-school vibe: tuxedoed waiters, a headwaiter who has worked there since opening day, and steak-and-lobster specialties. Though **Copley's** (621 North Palm Canyon Drive; 760-327-9555; copleyspalmsprings.com; $$$) might not have the culinary history of nearby Melvyn's Restaurant and Lounge, which opened as an inn in 1935, it has a different sort of storied past — it is housed in what was once Cary Grant's estate. It also has food that incorporates 21st-century flavors (one spring menu included dishes like a duck and artichoke salad with goat cheese, edamame, and litchi).

9 Toasting Friends 11 p.m.

The cocktail and microbrew crazes are still going strong in the desert, and the cavernous **Amigo Room** at the Ace Hotel (701 East Palm Canyon Drive; 760-325-9900; acehotel.com/palmsprings) remains at the front of the pack. In addition to pouring dozens of microbrews, the guys at the bar will measure, shake, and pour classic concoctions like the margarita and more offbeat options like the Figa (fig-infused vodka with Earl Grey and honey tangerine) that reek of late-night hipster cool. The mellow vibe, nightly entertainment (D.J.s, bands, bingo nights) and leather-banquette décor will keep you ordering.

SUNDAY

10 Get Close with Cactus 9 a.m.

Those looking for an early-morning calorie burn might prefer the uphill battles of Gastin or Araby Trail, but a hike through **Tahquitz Canyon** (500 West Mesquite Avenue; 760-416-7044; tahquitzcanyon. com), part of the natural oasis area called Indian Canyons, offers a leisurely alternative. A small entrance fee gets you access to a 1.8-mile loop and

the sights and smells that come with it: desert plants, lizards aplenty, and a stunning, 60-foot waterfall. Take a two-hour ranger-led tour or explore the trail at your own pace. You'll see arid desert and cool, palm-lined gorges.

11 *Pink Robots* Noon

For a one-of-a-kind experience that's both entertaining and eye-opening, drive out to the **Kenny Irwin Art and Light Show** (1077 East Granvia Valmonte; 760-774-8344; kennyirwinartist.com), a two-acre backyard sculpture park with massive, light-hearted, and very clever works that have to be seen to be believed. Metal and plastic junk from old vacuum cleaners to shopping carts is transformed

with welding and bright paint into giant robots, roller coasters, space vehicles, and even an intimidating version of Santa's sleigh. Visits are by appointment only, so be sure to call in advance.

OPPOSITE On tour in the Frey House II, which is built around a massive boulder. Designed by Albert Frey, it exemplifies the city's wealth of Modernist architecture.

ABOVE Hiking at Tahquitz Canyon.

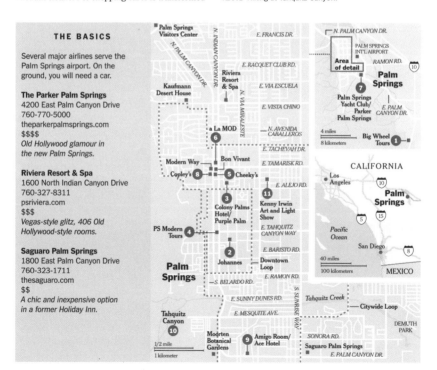

THE BASICS

Several major airlines serve the Palm Springs airport. On the ground, you will need a car.

The Parker Palm Springs
4200 East Palm Canyon Drive
760-770-5000
theparkerpalmsprings.com
$$$$
Old Hollywood glamour in the new Palm Springs.

Riviera Resort & Spa
1600 North Indian Canyon Drive
760-327-8311
psriviera.com
$$$
Vegas-style glitz, 406 Old Hollywood-style rooms.

Saguaro Palm Springs
1800 East Palm Canyon Drive
760-323-1711
thesaguaro.com
$$
A chic and inexpensive option in a former Holiday Inn.

Death Valley

Although Death Valley remains starkly dramatic, electricity, the automobile, and a reliable water supply have conspired to rob it of its terror. It is not what you would call a "pleasant" place, but it is a spectacularly beautiful one, containing typical and unusual Southwestern features in its manageable sprawl. (Death Valley National Park is nearly as large as Connecticut.) It can be hellishly hot in summer — the record is 134 degrees — and ice closes roads in the winter. But in spring and fall, the weather is cooperative. Drive up from Los Angeles, and you will begin by passing through Antelope Valley — where in early spring psychedelic California poppies may blanket the hills — and from there into the unexciting town of Mojave, once a center for borax shipments coming out of the valley. From this point on, things get really interesting. — BY MARK BITTMAN

FRIDAY

1 *Steep Descent* 5 p.m.

As you drive north up Interstate 395 toward **Death Valley National Park** (nps.gov/deva), you will see the Sierra Nevada and Mount Whitney, at nearly 15,000 feet the tallest peak in the contiguous United States, to the west, and a series of far smaller ranges to the east. But at **Olancha**, as you veer eastward on Highway 190, the landscape suddenly takes on an eerie air. Ahead is a barren, deep-orange mountain range, and to the right and left are salt plains, former lakes that shimmer in the late-afternoon light. This is Saline Valley, and it leads to the Argus Range, where a massive red-rocked canyon gapes below the road. Ahead lies a wide, stark valley, which turns out to be not Death Valley but Panamint Valley, and in any other part of the country it would be striking enough. Here, however, there is still the Panamint Range to cross and, after a climb to 5,000 feet, the steep descent begins; it will end at sea level on the floor of Death Valley.

2 *Overnight Oasis* 8 p.m.

Death Valley bares its geologic soul at every turn, and you will soon discover the kinds of details that make the desert delightful: the toughest plant life in the world, well-camouflaged wildlife, and a stunning array of rocks and minerals. If winter has been "wet" (that is, if rain has fallen at more than the usual

pace of two inches a year), spring brings carpets of wildflowers. Head to **Stovepipe Wells**, one of several oases in the park. You'll find a general store, a ranger station that is sometimes open, and **Stovepipe Wells Village**, a serviceable hotel. Dinner at the **Toll Road Restaurant** (760-786-2387; escapetodeathvalley.com; $$) includes some vegetarian options. Drinks are at the **Badwater Saloon**.

SATURDAY

3 *Multiple Sunrises* 6:30 a.m.

Dawn walks are guaranteed to be cool, and a stroll or hike in a canyon will give you several sunrises as the sun peeks above and dips below the upper reaches of the steep walls. **Mosaic Canyon**, in the foothills of Tucki Mountain, is just up the road and through a long alluvial fan. As in many of the park's canyons, you can drive right to the entrance and within minutes find near-pristine isolation. Here, the passage between the steep walls narrows to just a few feet, and you will immediately be engulfed by formations of mosaic and smooth, swirling, multicolored marble.

4 *Sculpted Sand* 10 a.m.

On the road to **Furnace Creek** are the valley's most accessible sand dunes. These look best (and

OPPOSITE A view of eroded hills from Zabriskie Point in Death Valley National Park.

BELOW A bullet-pocked backcountry road sign.

are at their coolest, of course), when the shadows are still long. For kids, the dunes will be the highlight of the trip, but their texture and beauty will excite everyone. Be prepared to get sandy as you wander barefoot, especially if it is breezy. Carry water — a must at all times in Death Valley. You can visit the original Stovepipe Well near here and, back on the road, you will pass Devil's Cornfield, an expanse of arrowweed whose dried stems resemble bundles of cornstalks.

5 *A History of Borax* Noon

The **Visitor Center & Museum** at Furnace Creek boasts a super collection of material about the area as well as exhibitions that will answer your rapidly accumulating questions about borax. (Should this not be enough, nearby are a borax museum with an impressive collection of machinery and wagons of 20-mule-team fame, and the semi-preserved Harmony Borax Works. Like it or not, chances are you will leave Death Valley a borax expert.) The human history of the valley is outlined here too, from its original known inhabitants, the Shoshones, to the unfortunate 49ers who stumbled into and named the valley while looking for a shortcut to the gold fields.

6 *The High and the Low* 1 p.m.

Have lunch at the **49'er Café** in the Ranch at Furnace Creek (furnacecreekresort.com; $$), which serves standard fare of salads, burgers, and pasta.

(In general, the food in Death Valley is not as bad as you might fear.) Then get directions for the 45-mile round trip down a dead-end road to the mile-high **Dante's View**, from which you can see both the highest (Mount Whitney) and lowest (Badwater, nearly 300 feet below sea level) points in the Lower 48.

7 *Panoramic Palette* 3 p.m.

Late in the afternoon is the best time to see central Death Valley's best-known and most beautiful spots: **Zabriskie Point** and the **Artist's Drive**. The former, thanks to the fame brought by the film of the same name, has a large parking lot and paved walkway to its top. From here there are panoramic views of the gently rounded golden hills nearby, a relatively friendly landscape compared with the stark, darkly colored Panamints in the background. Just down the road is the car-friendly visual highlight, **Artist's Palette**. These vast, multicolored hills, dominated by pink, green, and lavender, virtually pulsate in the soft light of late afternoon and early evening.

8 *Moonlight* 6 p.m.

Have a drink in the quietly tasteful lobby of the **Inn at Furnace Cree**k (furnacecreekresort.com) and then amble down to the **Wrangler Steakhouse** ($$$) at the Furnace Creek Ranch for dinner. Despite the name, steak is not the only option. If you're adventure-some — especially if there is a full moon — this is a

great time to tackle Golden Canyon. Otherwise, you will be tired enough to sleep, and there is plenty to do in the morning.

SUNDAY

9 *Stroll the Canyons* 7 a.m.

Golden Canyon is nestled among the hills seen from Zabriskie Point. Seventy-five years ago it was such a popular destination that a road was built through it. Now it is an easy hike — a stroll, really — that you can enjoy for a quarter of a mile or so, wandering in and out of the lovely side canyons, or take for a mile and a half, until you gain an open

OPPOSITE A campfire glowing against a black desert sky.

ABOVE A scene from Saline Road.

BELOW Hot springs at Saline Valley.

view of the red rocks of the **Red Cathedral** next to the yellow flank of Manley Beacon (you will see the Cathedral almost as soon as you get into the canyon).

10 *Option 1: Easy Exit* 9 a.m.

If you take the southern route out of the park, make a quick stop to gaze again at Artist's Drive, this time from the **Devil's Golf Course**, where the ground is a compacted mass of pure salt and mud. You can walk on it, but be careful: the crystals are sharp enough to cut you if you fall. A few miles down the road is **Badwater**, the lowest point in Death Valley (and the country), a terrifying expanse of salt fields and salt water, and a bitter disappointment to early travelers. Exit the park at Shoshone, and stop for a burger and a

root beer float at the **Crowbar Cafe & Saloon** (Highway 127, Shoshone; 760-852-4123; $$).

11 *Option 2: Rugged Detour* 9 a.m.

If you have time and a four-wheel drive vehicle, you may want to detour to the **Saline Valley Warm Springs**, a countercultural hangout since free spirits planted palms and built soaking tubs on its three levels of natural hot springs in the 1960s. The park took over in the '90s, but the "clothing optional" ethos still thrives, and a private group (salinepreservation. org) works with the park service. Stock up on fuel and supplies, and then, still just inside the park, turn north off Highway 190 onto a dirt road down into the valley. (It has traditionally been marked by a bullet-perforated "Road Closed" sign left from a long-ago winter.) Wrestle the washboard road for 53 miles. At the end, you'll find a mellow, relaxing scene and friendly people — often including families — bound by a love of the desert and its wide-open spaces.

ABOVE Remains of a tram line that hauled salt.

OPPOSITE The salt flats at Badwater Pool, the lowest point in the United States.

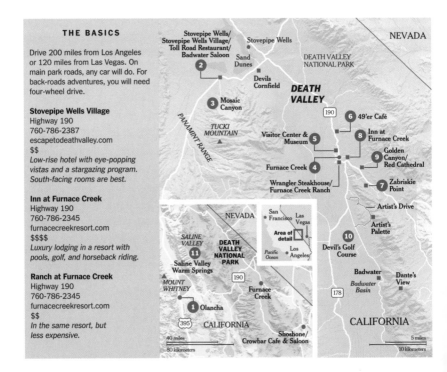

THE BASICS

Drive 200 miles from Los Angeles or 120 miles from Las Vegas. On main park roads, any car will do. For back-roads adventures, you will need four-wheel drive.

Stovepipe Wells Village
Highway 190
760-786-2387
escapetodeathvalley.com
$$
Low-rise hotel with eye-popping vistas and a stargazing program. South-facing rooms are best.

Inn at Furnace Creek
Highway 190
760-786-2345
furnacecreekresort.com
$$$$
Luxury lodging in a resort with pools, golf, and horseback riding.

Ranch at Furnace Creek
Highway 190
760-786-2345
furnacecreekresort.com
$$
In the same resort, but less expensive.

Stovepipe Wells/
Stovepipe Wells Village/
Toll Road Restaurant/
Badwater Saloon — Stovepipe Wells

NEVADA

Sand Dunes — DEATH VALLEY NATIONAL PARK

2

Devils Cornfield

DEATH VALLEY

3 Mosaic Canyon

PANAMINT RANGE

TUCKI MOUNTAIN

Visitor Center & Museum **5**

190 — **6** 49'er Café

8 Inn at Furnace Creek

9 Golden Canyon/ Red Cathedral

Furnace Creek **4**

Wrangler Steakhouse/ Furnace Creek Ranch

7 Zabriskie Point

— Artist's Drive

NEVADA

San Francisco • Las Vegas

Area of detail

Pacific Ocean — Los Angeles

Artist's Palette

SALINE VALLEY

DEATH VALLEY NATIONAL PARK

11 Saline Valley Warm Springs

MOUNT WHITNEY

190

Furnace Creek

Devil's Golf Course **10**

Badwater — Dante's View

Badwater Basin

178

1 Olancha

395 — CALIFORNIA

40 miles
80 kilometers

Shoshone/ Crowbar Cafe & Saloon

CALIFORNIA

5 miles
10 kilometers

Las Vegas

From a tourism perspective, Las Vegas is ever the chameleon. New restaurants, shows, clubs, and hotels are constantly reinventing Sin City with the aim of getting repeaters back to the tables. Big construction projects are always underway; the competition even extends to dueling Ferris wheels. But lately, projects have moved away from kitschy copies of foreign landmarks like an Egyptian pyramid in favor of celebrating Las Vegas's own swinging style, and there are even Vegas-compatible museums downtown. — BY ELAINE GLUSAC

FRIDAY

1 *Buy or Browse* 3 p.m.

Las Vegas shops make up a parade of high-end global brands designed to tempt high rollers. The **Crystals at CityCenter** mall (3720 Las Vegas Boulevard South; crystalsatcitycenter.com) exemplifies the mode with swimsuits from Eres, clothing from Stella McCartney, and accessories from Porsche Design. But the center, with sharp and soaring angles, designed by the architect Daniel Libeskind to resemble a quartz crystal, has an artistic side, too. Pick up a free CityCenter Fine Art walking tour brochure from the concierge at Aria or Vdara, the two neighboring resorts, for a self-guided tour of the public art collection in and around the building, including a sculpture by Henry Moore; *Big Edge*, a stack of boats wired in a web, by the artist Nancy Rubins; and several ice pillars that slowly melt each day, only to be refrozen each night, from the designers of the Bellagio fountains.

2 *Haute Perch* 6 p.m.

Since Wolfgang Puck arrived in 1992, celebrity chefs have flocked to the Strip. But most local observers agree that the food scene didn't really improve until the French guys arrived — the chefs Joël Robuchon and Guy Savoy, principally. Their namesake restaurants remain bastions of formality,

OPPOSITE The Las Vegas Strip, where ostentation can never be overdone.

RIGHT A performance of Cirque du Soleil's Beatles-based show at the Mirage.

but **L'Atelier de Joël Robuchon** (3799 Las Vegas Boulevard South; 702-891-7358; mgmgrand.com; $$$$), the 33-seat à la carte restaurant next door to Joël Robuchon in the MGM Grand, offers a more affordable meal and relaxed setting. Reserve a seat at the black granite bar to watch the chefs prepare dishes like quail stuffed with foie gras or steak tartare with frites.

3 *Circus Circuit* 9:30 p.m.

Move over, showgirls. The pervasive **Cirque du Soleil** performances — at several different hotels — and the mammoth ads everywhere make Cirque something like the Starbucks of the entertainment circuit here. Its Vegas extravaganzas have included shows based on the lives and music of Michael Jackson and the Beatles; the saga of a magical ringmaster visiting a haunted theater with trapeze artists, jump ropers, and strongmen; and the adult-themed *Absinthe*, with circus acts, some nudity, and lots of risqué humor. Tickets for all of the Cirque shows are available at cirquedusoleil.com.

SATURDAY

4 *Downward Dolphin* 8:30 a.m.

Las Vegas is a multitasking kind of town. It's only fitting, then, that while you practice yoga, you should

be able to watch dolphins. That's the combination offered in the hourlong **Yoga Among the Dolphins** at the Mirage Las Vegas (3400 Las Vegas Boulevard South; mirage.com). Students adopt yoga poses in a subterranean room with glass windows looking into the dolphin pools in Siegfried & Roy's Secret Garden and Dolphin Habitat. Curious bottlenose dolphins peer through the glass at you while you hold your Warrior I position.

5 *All That Glows* 11 a.m.

Before the Strip's Eiffel Tower replica and pseudo Manhattan skyline, Las Vegas marketed itself via neon signs. The **Neon Museum** (770 Las Vegas Boulevard North; 702-387-6366; neonmuseum.org)

celebrates the showy signage in a collection of more than 150 pieces, most still vibrant though not operational in their resting place in the outdoor "Neon Boneyard." Casino castoffs include signs from the Golden Nugget, Binion's, and the defunct Stardust and Moulin Rouge; a bright yellow duck that once advertised a used car lot; and a "Free Aspirin & Tender Sympathies" sign that was used to market a gas station. Book an hourlong guided tour; visitors are not allowed to wander here on their own.

6 *Made Men* 12:30 p.m.

The **Mob Museum** (300 Stewart Avenue; 702-229-2734; themobmuseum.org) covers a more notorious aspect of Las Vegas history. Occupying a 1933 former federal courthouse and post office where one of the anti-Mafia Kefauver Committee hearings was held, the Mob Museum lays out the history of organized crime across America with interactive exhibits, including the chance to simulate firing your own Tommy gun. Eventually it narrows its focus to Las Vegas, where a number

ABOVE AND LEFT The Crystals at CityCenter, designed by Daniel Libeskind to resemble a quartz crystal, takes the shopping mall to a new level in flamboyant Las Vegas style. Inside are shops including Tiffany's and Prada; a public art collection; and a Wolfgang Puck pizzeria.

of crime syndicates funneled their energies after legal crackdowns elsewhere. The tour through the three-story building thoughtfully offers the squeamish a chance to opt out of some of the more graphic galleries, featuring photos of mob hits, and winds up in a theater screening a documentary on Hollywood's fascination with gangsters.

7 *Go Fish* 2 p.m.

Estiatorio Milos (3708 Las Vegas Boulevard South; 702-698-7930; milos.ca/restaurants/las-vegas; $$$), a spinoff of the Greek seafood-focused restaurants run by the chef Costas Spiliadis in Montreal, New York, and other cities, is a mandatory midday stop, serving a three-course prix fixe lunch that manages to be relatively healthy in a town that equates fine dining with excess. Appetizer/entree/dessert combinations include dishes like a Greek mezze plate, grilled whole bass, and walnut cake. You'll eat well and still be ambulatory for the next stop.

8 *Dip or Strip* 4 p.m.

Poolside clubs known as day clubs have become the afternoon indulgence du jour at hotels up and down the Strip, primarily patronized by the trim and

toned under-30 set. At the **Aria Resort & Casino Las Vegas**, you can party with the bikini-clad, water-gun-armed crowds at the adults-only **Liquid Pool Lounge** (3730 Las Vegas Boulevard South; 702-693-8300; liquidpoollv.com). Or, for a quieter experience, seek serenity in the 81,000-square-foot **Spa & Salon at Aria** (aria.com), which has 62 treatment rooms, heated stone beds, a salt room, a steam room, a sauna, and an outdoor pool.

9 *Omakase Hour* 8 p.m.

The chef Nobu Matsuhisa and partners have their own hotel-within-a-hotel in a separate tower at Caesars Palace Hotel & Casino. Anchoring the Nobu Hotel just off the Caesars casino floor is a large branch of **Nobu** restaurants (3570 Las Vegas Boulevard South; 702-785-6677; nobucaesarspalace.com/restaurants.html; $$$$). Cushion-like fixtures that hang above the dining room like U.F.O.'s emit flattering light. The vast menu encompasses tiradito (Peruvian raw fish salad) and ceviche, wagyu steaks and brick-oven-baked chicken, skewered meats and, of course, sushi.

10 *Club House* 10 p.m.

There are limitless places to party in Las Vegas. For drinks overlooking the dancing fountains at the Bellagio resort, **Hyde** (3600 South Las Vegas Boulevard South; hydebellagio.com), designed in

ABOVE Blackjack tables at the Cosmopolitan. Gambling is still at the heart of it all.

LAS VEGAS

sleek style, morphs from sunset cocktail calm to late-night bash. **Hakkasan Las Vegas Restaurant and Nightclub** in the MGM Grand (3799 Las Vegas Boulevard South; hakkasanlv.com) sprawls over five levels of nightclubs and dancing.

SUNDAY

11 *Top Gear* 10:30 a.m.

In the city that sells itself on wish fulfillment, sitting behind the wheel of a high-performance car as it hurtles down a fast desert track is a perfect fit. **Speedvegas** (14200 Las Vegas Boulevard South;

702-874-8888; speedvegas.com) stables the latest exotic models, like the Ferrari 458 Italia and Lamborghini Aventador 102, designed to appeal to your inner F1 driver. The company used to organize driving trips to Red Rock Canyon 23 miles away, but the 50 m.p.h. speed limit felt too restrictive. So it built a 1.5-mile banked racetrack with 12 curves, 15 gear changes, and a straightaway where cars reach a top speed of 135 m.p.h.

ABOVE The Neon Museum celebrates a Las Vegas cliché, the bright, brash signs that light the nighttime on the Strip. In its collection are castoffs from casinos and oddities like a yellow duck that once advertised a used-car lot.

OPPOSITE A downsized Eiffel Tower and Arc de Triomphe at the Paris Las Vegas hotel. Gleaming in front is a desert extravagance, the Bellagio's pond.

THE BASICS

Las Vegas is a four-hour drive from Los Angeles. Its airport is served by the major airlines. Along the Strip, walk or use taxis, buses, and the monorail. Elsewhere, drive a car.

The Cosmopolitan
3708 Las Vegas Boulevard South
702-698-7000
cosmopolitanlasvegas.com
$$$
In a multibillion-dollar development, with hotel interiors designed by David Rockwell.

Aria Resort and Casino
3730 Las Vegas Boulevard South, in CityCenter
702-590-7111
aria.com
$$$
In CityCenter, with 4,000 rooms and every amenity (some with extra fees).

Santa Barbara

Santa Barbara may be tiny—its 90,000 residents could be seated in the Los Angeles Coliseum—but it packs Oprah-like cachet. Indeed, the billionaire media mogul and other A-listers have made this former outpost of Spain's American dominions their second home. Posh hotels, seven-figure mansions, and trendy boutiques have opened along the so-called American Riviera, catering to members of the Hollywood set who drive up every weekend to frolic among the languorous palms and suntanned celebrities. But don't let the crush of Ferraris and Prada fool you. With its perpetually blue skies and taco stands, Santa Barbara remains a laid-back town where the star attraction is still the beach.
— BY FINN-OLAF JONES

FRIDAY

1 *Lingering Glow* 5 p.m.

Santa Barbara's main beaches face southeast, but you can still catch the Pacific sunset by driving along Cliff Drive until it takes you to secluded **Hendry's Beach**. Hemmed by vertiginous cliffs that turn deep orange as the sun sets, the beach is popular with locals, surfers, and dolphins. Order a rum punch at the **Boathouse at Hendry's Beach** (2981 Cliff Drive; 805-898-2628; boathousesb.com), where you can still feel the warmth of the sun (or is it the fire pit?) long after it has set.

2 *Making Friends* 8 p.m.

Fresh California cuisine is the rule in this region of outstanding vineyards, luscious orchards, and right-off-the-boat seafood. Some of the freshest is at **Brophy Brothers Restaurant and Clam Bar** (119 Harbor Way; 805-966-4418; brophybros.com; $$$), which overlooks the harbor. Sit at the long communal table and strike up a conversation with your new friends. The night I was there, I was offered a job by a local developer. While I didn't take the job, I did sample the

OPPOSITE Sunset at Hendry's Beach. The main beaches in town face southeast, but at Hendry's the shore angles west, and the cliffs glow orange as the sun goes down.

RIGHT La Super Rica, pronounced by Julia Child to be the best of several good places in Santa Barbara to get a fresh and authentic homemade taco.

clam chowder ("The best in town," I was told about five times), followed by a terrific grilled swordfish with artichoke sauce. Hmmm, what was that starting salary again?

SATURDAY

3 *Bike to Brunch* 10 a.m.

Rent a bike at **Wheel Fun Rentals** (633 East Cabrillo Boulevard; 805-966-2282; wheelfunrentals.com) and roll along the ocean to the **East Beach Grill** (1118 East Cabrillo Boulevard; 805-965-8805; $), a greasy but bright breakfast institution popular with surfers, cyclists, and skaters, who swear by its banana wheat germ pancakes with eggs and bacon.

4 *Sacred Mission* 11:30 a.m.

It's hard not to feel awed when driving up the hill to **Mission Santa Barbara** (2201 Laguna Street; 805-682-4713; sbmission.org), a 1786 landmark with ocher-colored columns that is known as the Queen of the 21 original Spanish missions built along the California coastline. Escape the crowds by wandering outside in the flower-scented Sacred Garden. If there's a docent around, ask if you can see the glazed terra-cotta sculpture of St. Barbara watching over Mary and Jesus. A masterpiece from 1522, it was discovered three years ago in a storage

room that was being cleaned out. It is now installed in an alcove in the garden's private portico.

5 *Taco Heaven* 1 p.m.

Locals argue endlessly about the city's best taco joint. Julia Child threw her weight behind **La Super Rica** (622 North Milpas Street; 805-963-4940; $), ensuring perpetual lines for its homemade tortillas filled with everything from pork and cheese to spicy ground beans. **Lilly's** (310 Chapala Street; 805-966-9180; lillystacos.com; $), a tiny spot in the center of town run by the ever-welcoming Sepulveda family, serves tacos filled with anything from pork to beef eye. And **Palapa** (4123 State Street; 805-683-3074; palaparestaurant.com; $)

adds fresh seafood to the equation in its cheery patio just north of downtown, where the grilled sole tacos are fresh and light. Try all three places and join the debate.

6 *Paper Chase* 3 p.m.

Walt Disney's original will. A letter by Galileo. Lincoln's second Emancipation Proclamation (the 13th Amendment). The **Karpeles Manuscript Library and Museum** (21 West Anapamu Street; 805-962-5322; rain.org/~karpeles) was started by David Karpeles, a local real estate tycoon, and has one of the world's largest private manuscript collections. If this whets your appetite for collecting, wander seven blocks to **Randall House Rare Books** (835 Laguna Street; 805-963-1909; randallhouserarebooks.com), where the ancient tomes and rare documents have included a signed calling card from Robert E. Lee ($4,500) and the first official map of the State of California ($27,500).

ABOVE Sunset over the Pacific Ocean, viewed from the shore near the Santa Barbara Pier.

LEFT A guest room at San Ysidro Ranch, the longtime celebrity hangout where John F. Kennedy took his bride, Jacqueline, on their honeymoon.

OPPOSITE Two views of Mission Santa Barbara, known as the Queen of the original Spanish California missions.

7 *Shop Like the Stars* 5 p.m.

The main shopping drag, State Street, is filled with the usual chain stores like Abercrombie & Fitch. The consumerist cognoscenti head for the hills, to the Platinum Card district of **Montecito**, where you'll find local designers and one-off items along the eucalyptus-lined Coast Village Road. Highlights include **Antoinette** (No. 1046; 805-969-1515; antoinetteboutique.com), a mainstay for European designers working in the relaxed Santa Barbara style; **Angel** (No. 1221; 805-565-1599; wendyfoster. com), selling casual sportswear and accessories with a youthful vibe; and **Allora by Laura** (No. 1269; 805-563-2425; allorabylaura.com), a shiny, luxurious boutique featuring collections by Yigal Azrouël, Les Copains, and other designers.

8 *Celebrity Dining* 8 p.m.

J.F.K. and Jackie honeymooned there, Hollywood luminaries like Groucho Marx were regulars, and its 500 verdant acres have played host to guests ranging from Winston Churchill to Lucille Ball to Sinclair Lewis. The **San Ysidro Ranch** is one of the country's premier resorts, and its **Stonehouse** restaurant (900 San Ysidro Lane; 805-565-1700; sanysidroranch.com; $$$$) enjoys a similarly stellar reputation. Expect to see the T-shirt-with-blazer set sitting around an open fire while dining on dishes like warm mushroom salad, juniper-dusted venison loin,

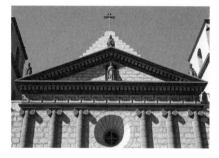

and fresh pastries. Take a post-dinner stroll around the terraced gardens where many of the ingredients were grown.

9 *Glamorous State* 11 p.m.

State Street heats up after 11 o'clock as college students and moneyed folk from the glittering hills descend to its bars and nightclubs. **Wildcat Lounge** (15 West Ortega Street; 805-962-7970; wildcatlounge.com), a retro bar with red-vinyl banquettes, is a place to mingle with the university crowd and local bohos grooving to house music. Cater-corner is **Tonic** (634 State Street; 805-897-1800; tonicsb.com), an airy dance club that draws students and recent graduates to its cabanas. The

international set heads to **Eos Lounge** (500 Anacapa Street; 805-564-2410; eoslounge.com) to dance in a packed, tree-shaded patio that looks like Mykonos on the Pacific.

SUNDAY

10 *Paging Moby-Dick* 10 a.m.

From December to February, some 30,000 gray whales migrate down the Pacific Coast from Alaska

to Baja California through a five-mile gap among the Channel Islands, a cluster of rocky isles 20 or so miles off the coast. Catch a glimpse of the commute — and see breaching whales rise from the sea around you — from the decks of the *Condor Express*, a high-speed catamaran that makes daily whale-watching trips (301 West Cabrillo Boulevard; 805-882-0088; condorexpress.com). Porpoises, sea lions, and the occasional killer whale join in on the fun.

ABOVE A signature Santa Barbara view: beach, pier, and the mountains that rise outside of town.

OPPOSITE Mission Santa Barbara dates to 1786.

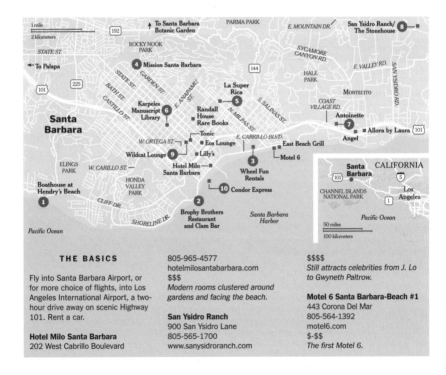

THE BASICS

Fly into Santa Barbara Airport, or for more choice of flights, into Los Angeles International Airport, a two-hour drive away on scenic Highway 101. Rent a car.

Hotel Milo Santa Barbara
202 West Cabrillo Boulevard

805-965-4577
hotelmilosantabarbara.com
$$$
Modern rooms clustered around gardens and facing the beach.

San Ysidro Ranch
900 San Ysidro Lane
805-565-1700
www.sanysidroranch.com

$$$$
Still attracts celebrities from J. Lo to Gwyneth Paltrow.

Motel 6 Santa Barbara-Beach #1
443 Corona Del Mar
805-564-1392
motel6.com
$-$$
The first Motel 6.

Carmel

With its architectural mishmash of storybook English cottages and Swiss Alpine chalets, the small California town of Carmel-by-the-Sea resembles a Disneyland version of Europe. You half expect a bereted Parisian to saunter out of one of the ridiculously cute Euro-themed bistros. But walk a few blocks to Carmel's steep, sandy beach and the view is pure California: a rugged Pacific coastline spangled with rocky outcroppings, ghostly cypress trees, and the electric green slopes of the famed Pebble Beach golf course. The one-square-mile village has no street lights, parking meters, or numbered addresses, but you wouldn't call it low-key. Once a bohemian outpost for people like Jack London, Carmel today is prime real estate, and the surrounding valley is abuzz with top-notch restaurants, boutique wineries, and upscale shops. — BY JAIME GROSS

FRIDAY

1 *Cocktails with Clint* 6 p.m.

Carmel has had its share of boldfaced residents, but few more enduring or beloved than Clint Eastwood, who was the town's mayor from 1986 to 1988 and still lives in the area. You might catch a glimpse of him at his restaurant at **Mission Ranch** (26270 Dolores Street; 831-624-6436; missionranchcarmel.com), his 22-acre property just outside of town, where he's been known to eat with his family and greet old-timers at the piano bar. Order a glass of wine and snag a seat on the heated restaurant patio overlooking a striking tableau: sheep meadows, rolling hills, and the shimmering ocean in the distance.

2 *California French* 8 p.m.

For an intimate dinner with plenty of foodie appeal, try **Aubergine** (Seventh Avenue and Monte Verde Street; 831-624-8578; auberginecarmel.com; $$$$), the award-winning restaurant at the Relais & Châteaux hotel L'Auberge Carmel. The menu changes daily, reflecting the availability of fresh local produce with dishes like roasted lamb with cranberry bean cassoulet.

OPPOSITE The Point Lobos State Reserve.

RIGHT A landscape painter at Bernardus Winery in vineyard country near Carmel-by-the-Sea.

SATURDAY

3 *Biking for a View* 8 a.m.

Beat the gawking motorists and entry fee for cars by waking early and biking the **17-Mile Drive**, the jaw-dropping corniche that hugs the rocky coastline between Carmel and Pacific Grove. **Adventures by the Sea** (299 Cannery Row, Monterey; 831-372-1807; adventuresbythesea.com) rents bikes and is an easy five miles from the drive's most scenic stretches, which are lined with sandy beaches, golf courses, and a 250-year-old cypress tree sprouting from a seaside boulder.

4 *Mission Museum* 11 a.m.

The **San Carlos Borroméo del Rio Carmelo Mission** (3080 Rio Road; 831-624-1271; carmelmission.org) was founded at its present site in 1771 by Father Junípero Serra and was once the headquarters for the entire California mission system. Known more simply as the Carmel Mission, the site includes a poppy-filled garden, an abalone-strewn cemetery, and a stone basilica with original 18th-century artworks. At the Mission's **Convento Museum**, you can peer into Father Serra's spartan living quarters — with a table, a chair, and a highly uncomfortable-looking wooden bed — and check out his book collection, identified as "California's first library."

5 *Lunch In-Town* 1 p.m.

Pick up lunch at Carmel's best food shops. **Bruno's Market and Deli** (Sixth Avenue and Junipero Avenue; 831-624-3821; brunosmarket.com) has gourmet tri-tip and barbecued chicken sandwiches. The **Cheese Shop** (Carmel Plaza, Ocean Avenue and Junipero Avenue, lower level; 800-828-9463; thecheeseshopinc.com) stocks picnic fixings, wine, and about 300 cheeses. They'll let you taste as many as you like, or they can assemble a customized cheese plate that you can nibble at the cafe tables out front.

6 *Poodles and Scones* 2 p.m.

In a town known for being dog-friendly, the **Cypress Inn** (Seventh Avenue and Lincoln Street; 831-624-3871; cypress-inn.com) takes the cake with poop bags at the door, bone-shaped biscuits at the front desk, and a *Best-in-Show*-worthy tea service. In addition to serving scones and crustless cucumber sandwiches, the tea service draws a head-spinning parade of Shih Tzus, toy poodles, and other impeccably groomed pups taking tea with their equally well-coiffed owners. Reservations are recommended.

7 *Stuff for Home* 4 p.m.

The 42 hidden courtyards and alleys of Carmel shelter a plethora of stylish galleries and fashionable boutiques. Spend a lazy afternoon wandering and browsing. One shop not to miss is the **Carmel Drug Store** (Ocean Avenue and San Carlos Street; 831-624-3819; carmeldrugstore.com), which has been selling handmade Swiss combs, grandma colognes, and Coca-Cola in glass bottles since 1910. Another high spot is the working studio and gallery of **Steven Whyte**, a local sculptor (Dolores Street

ABOVE The Cheese Shop stocks picnic fixings, wine, and about 300 different cheeses.

RIGHT A heron at Point Lobos State Reserve.

between Fifth and Sixth Avenues; 831-620-1917; stevenwhytesculptor.com) who makes hyper-realistic cast-bronze portraits.

8 *Casual Flavors* 8 p.m.

For dinner, make a beeline for one of Carmel's über-charming French or Italian restaurants. **La Bicyclette** (Dolores Street at Seventh Avenue; 831-622-9899; labicycletterestaurant.com; $$$) resembles a rustic village bistro. The compact menu spans Europe with dishes like beef with Gorgonzola-red wine sauce or German sausage with homemade sauerkraut. Also worth a try is **Cantinetta Luca** (Dolores Street between Ocean and Seventh Avenues; 831-625-6500; cantinettaluca.com; $$$), an Italian restaurant popular for its wood-fired pizzas, homemade pastas, predominantly Italian wine list, and a dozen types of salumi aged on site in a glass-walled curing room.

SUNDAY

9 *Sea Life* 11 a.m.

Legend has it that Robert Louis Stevenson hit on the inspiration for the 1883 novel *Treasure Island* while strolling the beach near Point Lobos. Retrace his steps at **Point Lobos State Reserve** (Route 1, three miles south of Carmel; 831-624-4909; pt-lobos.

parks.state.ca.us), a majestic landscape with 14 meandering trails. Don't forget binoculars: you can spot sea otters, seals, and sea lions year-round, and migrating gray whales December through May. Scuba divers take note: 60 percent of the reserve's 554 acres lies underwater, in one of the richest marine habitats in California. Scuba diving, snorkeling, and kayaking reservations can be booked through the park's website.

10 *Sip the Valley* 1 p.m.
Thanks to its coastal climate and sandy, loamy soil, Carmel Valley is gaining renown for its wines. Most of the tasting rooms are clustered in Carmel Valley Village, a small town with a handful of restaurants and wineries 12 miles east of Carmel-by-the-Sea. **Bernardus** (5 West Carmel Valley Road; 831-298-8021; bernardus.com), the granddaddy of

area wineries, is known for the breadth and quality of its wines. A relative newcomer, **Boekenoogen Wines** (24 West Carmel Valley Road; 831-659-4215; boekenoogenwines.com), is a small family-owned winery with a few varietals. Teetotalers can opt for a different kind of relaxation at **Bernardus Lodge** (415 West Carmel Valley Road; 831-658-3560; bernarduslodge.com). Its spa treatments have been known to include chardonnay facials.

ABOVE Cycling on the winding 17-Mile Drive, which hugs the rocky coastline between Carmel and Pacific Grove.

THE BASICS

Carmel-by-the-Sea is a scenic two-hour drive south of San Francisco.

L'Auberge Carmel
Seventh Avenue and Monte Verde Street
831-624-8578
laubergecarmel.com
$$$$
Winding staircases lead to 20 rooms, many with Japanese soaking tubs.

Cypress Inn
Seventh Avenue and Lincoln Street
831-624-3871
cypress-inn.com
$$$
Co-owned by Doris Day, whose songs are piped through the hotel.

Carmel Valley Ranch
1 Old Ranch Road
831-625-9500
carmelvalleyranch.com
$$$$
Fireplaces, terraces, golf course.

Sonoma County

If you're looking for a chocolate pinot noir sauce, keep driving. The rustic region of Sonoma County, California, may be a wine lovers' playground, but it lacks many of the touristy trappings of its more upscale and better-known neighbor, Napa. Not that Sonomans are complaining. Bumper stickers carry messages like "Kill Your TV" and "Subvert the Dominant Paradigm," and people here mean it. The freethinking tradition is being nurtured by a new generation of oenophiles who appreciate Sonoma's low-key charms, filling its beautiful historic towns with upscale boutiques, art galleries, and Old World-style restaurants. — BY KABIR CHIBBER

FRIDAY

1 *Young Blood* 4 p.m.

Wineries in Sonoma still tend to be small, young, and family-owned. One of the youngest is **Scribe Winery** (2300 Napa Road, Sonoma; 707-939-1858; scribewinery.com), started by Andrew Mariani and his family in 2007 on an estate of almost 200 acres that used to be a turkey farm. The winery, with its dusty driveway and artfully rundown hacienda, is so new the first wines from these vineyards—a pinot noir and chardonnay—could not be released until 2011. Early visitors to the winery tasted blends made from grapes grown nearby.

2 *Music in the Hills* 7 p.m.

Sonoma State is one of the smallest universities in the California system, but it boasts a world-class concert venue, the **Green Music Center** (1801 East Cotati Avenue, Rohnert Park; 866-955-6040; gmc.sonoma.edu), anchored by the 1,400-seat Weill Hall. Built of warm wood and featuring panoramic windows and bright acoustics, the hall plays host to the giants of classical music (Lang Lang, André Watts, the San Francisco Symphony). In the summer, popular, jazz, country, Broadway, and world music is performed for audiences on the lawn.

3 *Country and Town* 9 p.m.

Sondra Bernstein's restaurant serving "country food with French passion," **The Girl and the Fig** (110 West Spain Street, Sonoma; 707-938-3000; thegirlandthefig.com; $$-$$$), is an institution. Dishes

like pork belly tartine with pickled green tomatoes are available until 11. In downtown Petaluma, **Speakeasy** (Helen Putnam Plaza, 139 Petaluma Boulevard North; 707-776-4631; speakeasypetaluma.com; $$), a laid-back late-hour spot with an alleyway patio, specializes in old-timey cocktails and inventive spins on small plates like lobster mac and cheese and couscous tagine.

SATURDAY

4 *Farmer's Choice* 10 a.m.

A bit too early to be an oenophile? Luckily, there's much more to Sonoma than wine. The local food movement is long-established here, and Sonomans are as passionate about what they eat as what they drink. Sample the locally produced cheeses and kefirs using goat's milk at **Redwood Hill Farm** (2064 Highway 116 North, Sebastopol; 707-823-8250; redwoodhill.com) and organic wildflower honey from **Quivira Vineyards & Winery** (4900 West Dry Creek Road, Healdsburg; 707-431-8333; quivirawine.com). And **La Michoacana** (18495 Highway 12, Sonoma; 707-938-1773) makes

OPPOSITE Sonoma, a wine region of low-key charms.

BELOW A familiar sight on Sonoma Valley winery tours: an open-air table overlooking a vineyard.

soft, creamy ice creams with flavors like caramel and mango, just like those found in Tocumbo, Mexico, where the owner, Teresita Carr, grew up.

5 *Canvases and Fans* 12:30 p.m.

Healdsburg, one of Sonoma's main towns, is full of boutiques and second homes of the San Francisco Bay Area's beautiful and wealthy, but it retains a youthful vibe. It also has a sizable collection of modern art. The **Healdsburg Center for the Arts** (130 Plaza Street; 707-431-1970; healdsburgcenterforthearts.com) features a rotating cast of local and regional artists, while **Hawley Tasting Room and Gallery** (36 North Street; 707-473-9500; hawleywine.com) displays the landscape paintings of Dana Hawley, who is the wife of the respected local winemaker John Hawley. The **Capture Gallery** (105 Plaza Street; 707-431-7030; capturefineart.com) has high-end photography of the Sonoma terrain. And don't leave without checking out the **Hand Fan Museum** (219 Healdsburg Avenue; 707-431-2500; handfanmuseum.com), the first in the country dedicated to the once popular accessory.

6 *The Padrino (of Wine)* 2:30 p.m.

Around here, Francis Ford Coppola is known more as a winemaker than as an Oscar-winning director, having been a vintner for decades at the Rubicon Estate in Napa. In 2010 Coppola opened the **Francis Ford Coppola Winery** in Sonoma (300 Via Archimedes, Geyserville; 707-857-1471; franciscoppolawinery.com). The 88-acre estate has a restaurant called Rustic featuring some of Coppola's favorite dishes, two outdoor swimming pools to keep things child-friendly, and Hollywood memorabilia like Vito Corleone's desk from *The Godfather*. Best of all, some tastings of standard wines are free — a rarity in California.

7 *Bubble Bath* 5:30 p.m.

Sonoma has its fair share of high-end resorts for feeling sequestered from the world. But it's better to take advantage of the excellent day spas in the area that let you pop in and out at your leisure. **A Simple Touch Spa** (239C Center Street, Healdsburg; 707-433-6856; asimpletouchspa.com) specializes in aromatherapy baths and relaxing massage. The stylish spa at **Hotel Healdsburg** (25 Matheson Street, Healdsburg; 707-431-2800; hotelhealdsburg.com) has a reviving body wrap using wine and local honey.

8 *Polished Classics* 7 p.m.

In 2004, when the French chef Bruno Tison took over the restaurant **Santé** at the historic **Fairmont Sonoma Mission Inn and Spa** (100 Boyes Boulevard, Sonoma; 707-938-9000; fairmont.com/sonoma; $$$), he set his sights high, with a creative menu that paired French flavors with American favorites. The gamble seems to have paid off: the restaurant received a Michelin star in 2009 — one of only four in Sonoma County to be awarded the distinction. Expect dishes like macaroni and cheese with Maine lobster and black truffles, or roasted duck breast in a "dirty rice" of mushrooms and foie gras, accompanied by a duck confit. There's an extensive selection of regional wines.

9 *Cocktail Tasting* 10 p.m.

Wine country is not renowned for its night life, but that doesn't mean you can't have fun. The cocktail bar at the sleek and minimalist **El Dorado**

ABOVE At the Francis Ford Coppola Winery, taste the vintages made by the renowned film director. Then pop into the Movie Gallery for a look at props like the Godfather's desk and this Tucker car.

Hotel (405 First Street West, Sonoma; 707-996-3220; eldoradosonoma.com) exudes an effortless glamour and gets particularly lively during the Sonoma Jazz Festival. Try the peach jalapeño, a mix of peppers and peach vodka. The town of Santa Rosa is also filled with bars, though many can feel fratty. An exception is the retro **Lounge at the Flamingo Resort** (2777 Fourth Street, Santa Rosa; 707-528-8530; flamingoresort.com/entertainment), where couples dance to live music in a variety of genres.

SUNDAY

10 *Salt Air* 9 a.m.

Leave the vineyards behind and head to the coast, about an hour away at Bodega Bay. **Campbell Cove**, by the Bodega Head, is a secluded beach that feels as though it was made just for you and the seagulls. Spend some time on the sand and chill. Then take a little time to drive up a few miles along the rugged Sonoma coast.

11 *Yeast Notes* Noon

Tired of pondering the finer points of merlot versus pinot noir? Well, get ready to debate the terroir of malted barley and hops at Sonoma's microbreweries. **Dempsey's** (50 East Washington Street, Petaluma; 707-765-9694; dempseys.com) has a stout called Ugly Dog — because the annual World's Ugliest Dog Contest is held in town. **Bear Republic Brewing Co.** (345 Healdsburg Avenue, Healdsburg; 707-433-2337; bearrepublic.com) serves a pale ale called Crazy Ivan that's been mixed with a yeast used by Trappist monks.

THE BASICS

Sonoma is about an hour's drive north of San Francisco.

Sonoma Creek Inn
239 Boyes Boulevard, Sonoma
707-939-9463
sonomacreekinn.com
$$
Combines the feel of a bed-and-breakfast with a 1950s-style motel.

H2hotel
219 Healdsburg Avenue, Healdsburg
707-922-5251
h2hotel.com
$$$
Minimalist style of white linens and bamboo floors.

Ledson Hotel
480 First Street East, Sonoma
707-996-9779
ledsonhotel.com
$$$$
Marble showers and whirlpool tubs in all six rooms.

San Francisco

San Francisco typically wows visitors with its heights. The hills sear themselves into memory after a few up-and-down-and-up-again cable car rides or punishing walks. Then there are the hilltop sights: the sweeping vistas and the picturesque Victorians. But surrounding all of that is coastline, miles of peninsula shore along the Pacific Ocean and the expansive natural harbor of San Francisco Bay. Once a working industrial area with pockets of outright blight, much of the city's waterfront has been polished into another of its pleasures. To sample what it offers, start exploring in the east, south of the Bay Bridge, and loop your way west to the Golden Gate and then south to Ocean Beach. In one weekend romp, you'll join San Franciscans in many of the places they love best — and see what remains of their city's maritime heart.
— BY JESSE MCKINLEY

FRIDAY

1 *A Ride Along the Water* 4 p.m.

China Basin, south of the Bay Bridge, is home to an entirely new neighborhood since big changes began around 2000. The University of California, San Francisco, has developed its **Mission Bay Campus**, adding handsome new buildings and public art including two soaring steel towers by Richard Serra, a San Francisco native. And the opening of **AT&T Park**, the baseball field that's home to the San Francisco Giants, brought new energy and new monuments, including tributes to greats like Willie Mays and Willie McCovey (the basin is often called McCovey Cove). Rent a bike at the **Bike Hut**, a nonprofit outlet at Pier 40 (415-543-4335; thebikehut.org), and pedal the wide promenade along the water.

2 *Embarcadero Imbibing* 5:30 p.m.

Once the home to a raised freeway — demolished after the 1989 Loma Prieta earthquake — and before that a busy wharf area receiving cargo from around

the world, the **Embarcadero** is now one of San Francisco's most inviting Friday night spots, filled with workweek-wearied downtown workers ready to relax. Two inviting spots for a drink and appetizers are **Waterbar** (399 Embarcadero; 415-284-9922; waterbarsf.com) and **Epic Steak** (369 Embarcadero; 415-369-9955; epicsteak.com). Views of the Bay Bridge are unbeatable at either, but oysters at Waterbar can really set the mood.

3 *Boat to a Bistro* 8 p.m.

Forbes Island (off Pier 39; 415-951-4900; forbesisland.com; $$$) is not an island, but it is an experience. Created from a 700-ton houseboat, it's a floating restaurant complete with an underwater dining room (with portholes), a 40-foot lighthouse, and an outdoor bar within barking distance of local sea lions. Its nautically minded creator and owner, Forbes Thor Kiddoo, pilots the pontoon boat that brings patrons from a nearby pier. The fish chowder is briny and yummy, as is an assortment of turf (including flat steak in a cognac cream sauce) and surf (organic salmon). Kiddoo, a houseboat designer who combines Gilligan's mirth with the Skipper's physique, is a charming host. Don't miss the 360-degree view from the top of the lighthouse; it may be the best — and the most unusual — vantage point in the city.

OPPOSITE Rocks and surf below the Golden Gate Bridge.

RIGHT Waterbar offers cool drinks, tasty oysters, and a sweeping view of San Francisco Bay and the San Francisco-Oakland Bay Bridge.

SATURDAY

4 *Flip, Flop, Fly* 9 a.m.

Yearning for a Saturday-morning workout? Go for a run at **Crissy Field**, once a waterfront airfield and now San Francisco's weekend outdoor gym, with masses of joggers, walkers, and cyclists cruising its paths. It's part of the **Presidio**, formerly a military complex guarding San Francisco Bay and the strategic strait at its entrance — the Golden Gate. Now it's all part of the Golden Gate National Recreation Area. Activities run from the quirky (crabbing classes at the Civil War-era Fort Point, under the Golden Gate Bridge) to the caffeinated (outdoor coffee at the **Beach Hut**, 1199 East Beach; 415-561-7761). But the bounciest option is the **House of Air** (926 Mason Street; 415-345-9675; houseofair. com), a trampoline center in one of the repurposed buildings on the main Presidio post. Flanked by a kids' swimming school and an indoor climbing center, the House of Air also features training classes, a trampoline dodgeball court, and a bouncy castle for tots.

5 *Chow Time* Noon

Dining at the Presidio has come a long way since the days of reveille at dawn. Several restaurants now dot the northeastern corner, where much of the Presidio's development has occurred since it

was transferred to the National Park Service in the mid-1990s. One spot that retains the old military feel is the **Presidio Social Club** (563 Ruger Street; 415-885-1888; presidiosocialclub.com; $$$). As unpretentious as an Army grunt, the club offers old-time drinks (the rye-heavy Sazerac, which dates to 1840) and a pleasantly affordable brunch. A dessert of beignets with hot cocoa can fuel you up for your next offensive.

6 *Inner Sunset Stroll* 2 p.m.

Detour off base to the Inner Sunset neighborhood and **Green Apple Books on the Park** (1231 Ninth Avenue; 415-742-5833; greenapplebooks.com). Don't be fooled by the narrow storefront; the shop reaches far into the interior space, and is big enough to be anchored by a dedicated children's area. Like its sister store — the venerable Green Apple Books, opened in 1967 — it also hosts events featuring an impressive lineup of writers. Afterward, stroll down the street and into **Urban Bazaar** (1371 Ninth Avenue; 415-664-4422; urbanbazaarsf.com) to browse fair-trade and quirky, locally made gifts.

7 *Nature and Art* 4 p.m.

Take a walk through the hills and woods on the Pacific coast side of the Presidio, where miles of hiking trails lead to scenic overlooks (presidio.gov). You may also find an artwork or two. The Presidio doesn't need much help being beautiful, but that hasn't stopped artists who have placed installations and sculpture on the grounds. One is Andy Goldsworthy, an environmental British sculptor whose ephemeral pieces in the park include *Spire* — a soaring wooden spike — and *Wood Line*, a serpentine forest-floor sculpture made of eucalyptus.

8 *Burning, Man* 6:30 p.m.

Few things say California more than beach bonfires, a proud tradition up and down the coast. In San Francisco, free spirits keep it going at **Ocean Beach**, the wide sand expanse south of Baker Beach (the spot where Burning Man, the now Nevada-based arts fest,

OPPOSITE At Crissy Field, a part of the Presidio, masses of joggers, walkers, and cyclists cruise the paths.

BELOW *Spire*, a sculpture by Andy Goldsworthy, at the Presidio. Miles of trails lead to ocean views.

was born). While the wind can be biting, the mood at the impromptu fires is usually warm as groups congregate with guitars, pipes, and good vibes. This is the only beach in the city that permits bonfires, and under Golden Gate National Recreation Area rules, they must be extinguished by 9. So while bonfires go at any hour of the day, this is the classic time. Take a blanket and a pullover and watch the sunset, surf, and sparks collide.

9 *Dinner at the Edge* 8 p.m.

The **Cliff House** (1090 Point Lobos; 415-386-3330; cliffhouse.com) has been serving visitors at the end of the continent since the Civil War, and it is still perched on the same rocks, facing shark-fin-shaped Seal Rock and the crashing waves below. The **Bistro** ($$), upstairs, serves entrees and cocktails like the Ramos Fizz, a gin drink — and purported hangover cure — made with egg whites, half-and-half, and orange juice. Downstairs is the higher-end **Sutro's**

($$$), where the specialties include a two-crab sandwich and grilled scallops.

SUNDAY

10 *Other Side of the Park* 11 a.m.

The western edge of **Golden Gate Park**, facing Ocean Beach, has a Rodney Dangerfield feel, less known and appreciated than the park's cityside flanks. But its offerings are impressive, including a cheap and public nine-hole, par-3 golf course, a

lovely bison enclave, and serene fly-fishing ponds. A good place to convene for any park adventure is the **Park Chalet** (1000 Great Highway; 415-386-8439; parkchalet.com; $$$). In this somewhat hidden spot just off Ocean Beach, kids run free in the wilds of the park and parents enjoy a brunch buffet that advertises "bottomless champagne."

ABOVE The skyline, with San Francisco Bay in the background. A city of hills, valleys, and sea, San Francisco abounds in gorgeous views.

OPPOSITE A 21st-century addition, *Cupid's Span*, by Claes Oldenburg and Coosje van Bruggen, frames a view of the Ferry Building clock tower, a more traditional San Francisco landmark.

THE BASICS

Take the BART train from San Francisco International Airport to downtown. Get around the city using taxis and public transportation.

Hotel Vitale
8 Mission Street
415-278-3700
hotelvitale.com
$$$$
Style and luxury on the Embarcadero, across from the landmark Ferry Building.

Harbor Court Hotel
165 Steuart Street
415-882-1300
harborcourthotel.com
$$
Boutique hotel with bay views.

Union Street Inn
2229 Union Street
415-346-0424
unionstreetinn.com
$$$
Quiet and charming bed-and-breakfast.

Indexes

PAGE 2 Los Angeles at night.

THE BASICS

A brief informational box for the destination, called "The Basics," appears with each *36 Hours* article in this book. The box provides some orientation for that location; for instance, whether a traveler arriving by plane should rent a car to follow the itinerary. "The Basics" also recommends two or three reliable hotels or other lodgings.

PRICES

Since hotel and restaurant prices change quickly, this book uses a system of symbols, based on 2016 United States dollars.

Hotel room, standard double:
Budget, up to $125 per night: $
Moderate, $126 to $250: $$
Expensive, $251 to $375: $$$
Luxury, $376 and above: $$$$

Restaurants, dinner entree:
Budget, up to $15: $
Moderate, $16 to $30: $$
Expensive, $31 to $45: $$$
Very Expensive, $46 and up: $$$$

Restaurants, full breakfast, or lunch entree:
Budget, up to $10: $
Moderate, $11 to $20: $$
Expensive, $21 to $30: $$$
Very Expensive, $31 and up: $$$$

Acknowledgments

We would like to thank everyone at *The New York Times* and at TASCHEN who contributed to the creation of this book.

Special recognition must go to Nina Wiener, Eric Schwartau, and Anne Sauvadet, the dedicated editors behind the scenes at TASCHEN, and to Nazire Ergun; to Natasha Perkel and Barbara Berasi, the *Times* artists whose clear and elegantly crafted maps help to make the itineraries comprehensible for the reader and traveler; to *Times* photo editors Phyllis Collazo and Evan Sklar; and to Olimpia Zagnoli, whose illustrations introduce and enliven every article.

Guiding the transformation of newspaper material to book form at TASCHEN were Josh Baker and Marco Zivny, art directors; Philipp Sendner, production manager; and Lindsey Dole, David Knowles, Jonathan Newhall, Robert Noble, Mari Rustan, and Sarah Wrigley.

Jeff Z. Klein fact-checked and updated the manuscript. Heidi Giovine helped keep production on track at critical moments.

But the indebtedness goes much further back, and deeper into the *New York Times* staff and the list of the newspaper's many contributors. This book grew out of the work of all of the editors, writers, photographers, and others whose contributions and support for the weekly *36 Hours* column built a rich archive over many years.

For this legacy, credit must go first to Stuart Emmrich, who created the column in 2002 and then refined the concept over eight years, first as the *Times* Escapes editor and then as Travel editor. Without his vision, there would be no *36 Hours*. His successors in the role of Travel editor, Danielle Mattoon and then Monica Drake, have brought steady leadership to the column and support to the *36 Hours* books.

Suzanne MacNeille, the direct editor of *36 Hours* at *The Times*, and her predecessors, Denny Lee and Jeff Z. Klein, have guided *36 Hours* superbly through the world by assigning and working with writers, choosing and assigning destinations, and assuring that the weekly column would entertain and inform readers while upholding *Times* journalistic standards. As Escapes editors, Amy Virshup and Mervyn Rothstein saw the column through many of its early years, assuring its consistent quality.

The talented *Times* photo editors who have overseen images and directed the work of photographers for *36 Hours* include Phaedra Brown, Lindsay Blatt, Jessica De Witt, Lonnie Schlein, Gina Privitere, Darcy Eveleigh, Laura O'Neill, Chris Jones, and the late John Forbes.

Among the many editors on the *Times* Travel and Escapes copy desks who have kept *36 Hours* at its best over the years, three who stand out are Florence Stickney, Steve Bailey, and Carl Sommers. Fact-checkers for the weekly column have included John Dorman, Emily Brennan, and Rachel Lee Harris.

Finally, we must offer a special acknowledgment to Benedikt Taschen, whose longtime readership and interest in the *36 Hours* column led to the partnership of our two companies to produce this book.

— BARBARA IRELAND AND ALEX WARD

Editor Barbara Ireland
Project management Alex Ward
Photo editor Phyllis Collazo and Evan Sklar
Maps Barbara Berasi and
Natasha Perkel
Spot illustrations Olimpia Zagnoli
Editorial coordination Nina Wiener and
Anne Sauvadet
Art direction Marco Zivny and Josh Baker
Layout and design Marco Zivny
Production Philipp Sendner

EACH AND EVERY TASCHEN BOOK PLANTS A SEED!
TASCHEN is a carbon neutral publisher. Each year, we offset our annual carbon emissions with carbon credits at the Instituto Terra, a reforestation program in Minas Gerais, Brazil, founded by Lélia and Sebastião Salgado. To find out more about this ecological partnership, please check: www.taschen.com/zerocarbon
Inspiration: unlimited. Carbon footprint: zero.

©2016 TASCHEN GmbH
Hohenzollernring 53, D–50672 Köln
www.taschen.com

ISBN 978-3-8365-3942-5 Printed in Italy

YOU CAN FIND
TASCHEN STORES
IN

Beverly Hills
354 N. Beverly Drive

Hollywood
Farmers Market
6333 W. 3rd Street

Miami
1111 Lincoln Road

New York
107 Greene Street

"If browsing is considered an art form, the TASCHEN store is a masterpiece." — *Dwell*

TRUST *THE NEW YORK TIMES* WITH YOUR NEXT 36 HOURS

AROUND THE WORLD...

"An elegant ... planning tool and beautifully photographed coffee-table book."

—FORBES.COM, *NEW YORK*

WORLD
3/36/365

ACROSS A CONTINENT...

USA & CANADA

EUROPE

LATIN AMERICA & THE CARIBBEAN

ASIA & OCEANIA

USA & CANADA EAST

USA & CANADA WEST

OR IN YOUR FAVORITE CITY...

"Great for both ambitious jetsetters and ambling couch surfers."

—COOLHUNTING.COM

LOS ANGELES

NEW YORK

LONDON
(COMING SOON)

FOR NEWS ON UPCOMING BOOKS IN THIS SERIES, VISIT TASCHEN.COM/36HOURS